INTRODUCTION TO

LAW FIRM PRACTICE

MICHAEL DOWNEY

Partner, Hinshaw & Culbertson LLP
Adjunct Professor, Washington University School of Law

ABA
AMERICAN BAR ASSOCIATION
Law Practice Division

Commitment to Quality: The Law Practice Management Section is committed to quality in our publications. Our authors are experienced practitioners in their fields. Prior to publication, the contents of all our books are rigorously reviewed by experts to ensure the highest quality product and presentation. Because we are committed to serving our readers' needs, we welcome your feedback on how we can improve future editions of this book.

Cover design by Kelly Book, ABA Publishing.

Printed in the United States of America.

Library of Congress Cataloging-in-Publication Data

Downey, Michael P.
Introduction to law firm practice / by: Michael Downey.
p. cm.
Includes index.
ISBN 978-1-60442-824-7
1. Law firms—United States. 2. Law offices—United States. 3. Practice of law—United States. I. Title.
KF300.D69 2010
340.068—dc22

2010005662

Discounts are available for books ordered in bulk. Special consideration is given to state bars, CLE programs, and other bar-related organizations. Inquire at Book Publishing, American Bar Association, 321 N. Clark Street, Chicago, Illinois 60654.

Dedication

To Beth, my wife and friend—definitely my better half.

Contents

Acknowledgments

This book stands on the shoulders of many law practice management gurus and mentors. I do not have the time, space, or ability to recognize them all. Nevertheless, I want to acknowledge some of the people who helped bring this book to fruition:

- The ABA Law Practice Management Section and its leadership and staff, in particular Tim Johnson, Denise Constantine, Trish Cleary, and Kimia Shelby of LPM Publishing; and Joan Bullock, who oversaw this project for the LPM Publishing Board;
- Colleagues at Hinshaw, in particular practice group mentors Tom Browne, Anthony Davis, Peter Jarvis, Ron Mallen, Tom McGarry, Frances O'Meara, and Tom Sukowicz; Paul Boken; Teri Drew; Jeff Glass; Jamie Schwab; Josh Vincent; Marilyn Yeager; David Grossbaum for his review of materials regarding professional liability insurance; and Dusty Holoubek and Katie McCormack for their help with marketing and online resources;
- Professors at George Washington University's Law Firm Management Program, in particular Stephen Chitwood, Jim Jones, Carl Leonard, and William Johnston;
- Students and faculty at Washington University School of Law, in particular Dorsey Ellis, Dan Keating, and Tomea Mayer Mersmann;

- Art Garwin in the ABA Center for Professional Responsibility for his review of all references to the ethics rules;
- Numerous mentors and colleagues in the law, including Ron Fox, John Galvin, Sherry Hurst, Bart Sullivan, and Jeanne Timme of Fox Galvin LLC; David Fleisher, Michael Kahn, and Eric Martin of Bryan Cave LLP; Robert Owen of Fulbright & Jaworski LLP; Chip Misko of Stinson Morrison Hecker LLP; Maggie Telford; Don Downing of Gray Ritter & Graham, P.C.; and Ed Cohen and Chris Hohn of Thompson Coburn LLP;
- My father Greg Downey, CPA, for his guidance on finance issues, and my mother Jeanne Downey, for proofing the entire text (twice); and
- My wife Beth and children Andy, Liam, and Katie, who have sacrificed much for this book and my practice.

Finally, any mistakes that remain in the text are the author's alone.

About the Author

Michael Downey

Michael Downey is a partner in the national lawyer ethics and risk management practice group at Hinshaw & Culbertson LLP, a law firm with approximately 500 lawyers and offices in twelve states. At Hinshaw, Mr. Downey focuses his practice on advising lawyers, accountants, and their firms on professional ethics, business, and risk management issues. He also handles litigation—primarily for lawyers and accountants—and disciplinary proceedings. Before joining Hinshaw, Mr. Downey practiced as a partner at a St. Louis litigation boutique, primarily representing global oil and pharmaceutical companies, and as a litigation associate at a large regional firm.

In addition to his law practice, Mr. Downey has served as an adjunct professor at Washington University School of Law since 2001. Courses taught include legal ethics and law firm practice. He also taught legal ethics at St. Louis University School of Law.

An author of more than 40 articles, Mr. Downey presented more than 200 times on legal ethics and law firm practice. He has been interviewed widely, including by the *ABA Journal*, *American Lawyer*, *National Law Journal*, and *Wall Street Journal*. He has also been quoted on the front page of the *New York Times* and appeared as a guest on NPR's *Talk of the Nation*. He blogs at **www.theEthicalQuandary.com**.

Mr. Downey has held numerous leadership positions in national, state, and local bar associations. He chaired the Ethics & Technology Committee in the ABA Center for Professional Responsibility and serves on the Section Council of the ABA Law Practice Management Section. He also served on the Missouri Bar's Ethics 2005 Committee and Special Committee on Lawyer Advertising and chaired the Illinois State Bar Association's Standing Committee on Professional Conduct.

Mr. Downey graduated with honors from Georgetown University and first in his class from Washington University School of Law, then clerked for the Hon. Pasco M. Bowman, Chief Judge of the U.S. Court of Appeals for the Eighth Circuit, before entering private practice. In 2006, he earned a certificate in Law Firm Management from George Washington University.

Mr. Downey invites your comments or questions. He can be reached in Hinshaw's St. Louis office at (314) 241-2600 or by email at **mdowney@hinshawlaw.com**.

Additional information and materials are available at **www.DowneyonLawPractice.com**.

Introduction

Most young lawyers join a private law practice after law school graduation.[1] Many of them do so with only limited information about how a law firm works—or how they can act to maximize their chances for success at a law firm.

This book is intended to draw back the curtain and reveal how law firms operate. This exercise is not intended to embarrass firms; rather, it is to expose reality. Such revelation should help newer entrants to law firms better understand the private law firm environment. The primary goal is to empower better decision-making, and thus help newer entrants find greater satisfaction and happiness in a law firm.

In writing this book, I faced four major challenges. First, to provide a basic understanding of law firms and their operations, this book tackles a large number of significant subjects, ranging from law firm operations and profitability to work assignments, from marketing to risk management. The number and breadth of such topics makes comprehensive treatment impossible. Many of

[1]Since 1993, the percentage of law school graduates taking their first job at a private law firm has hovered at between 55 and 58 percent. *See* National Association of Law Placement (NALP) Press Release, *Market for New Law Graduates Up—Topping 90% for First Time Since 2000, available at* **http://www.nalp.org/press/details.php?id=70**. Only about 21 percent of 2006 graduates started at firms with more than 100 lawyers. *See id.*

the topics discussed in this book deserve and are themselves the subject of separate books and even multi-book treatises.

Second, although newer lawyers (and even many senior lawyers) may believe that all law firms are essentially the same, private law firms are extremely diverse. There are almost 170,000 different law offices and firms in the United States that employ more than a million people.[2] These firms range from solo practitioners in one-person offices to firms with 3,500 lawyers and thousands of support staff. I address broad swaths of the legal profession, but cannot and do not describe every variation of firm or legal practice.

Third, American law firms are privately-owned institutions. They are not required to publish shareholder or other financial or annual reports. Many guard information regarding their operations very carefully. Much of the information that I use in preparing this text is what I could find publicly, including in news reports. This tends to create a bias, however, toward information concerning larger firms.

Fourth, for reasons including some discussed in this book, law firms are often not optimally managed. This book is not intended to serve as and should not be used as a "best practices" manual. Rather, this book is intended to provide an overview and selection of what law firms are and how they actually function—not how they ideally should function. This way, a new lawyer or law firm employee can understand the surroundings and be successful, however that lawyer or law firm employee might define success.

This book seeks to walk a line between being too advanced and too basic. It tries to provide advanced insights that will help the reader understand the inner workings of law firms and information about what the senior lawyers are experiencing or doing—even if the senior lawyers or managers cannot put their experiences or activities into words. But this book also tries to address basic information so that the reader will understand the basic formations and operations of a law firm

Four experiences have prepared me to write this book. First, I have now practiced at law firms for more than a decade. Includ-

[2]2002 Economic Census, Professional, Scientific, and Technical Services.

ing summer clerkships during law school, I have worked at four firms with between 10 and almost 500 lawyers. Each of these firms had different personalities and practices, and those personalities and practices shifted over time. Thus, I write drawing upon rich personal experience at law firms.

Second, I have been a formal student in the management and operation of law firms. In particular, in 2006 I completed the Law Firm Management graduate certificate program at George Washington University. This program was co-sponsored by and taught by consultants from Hildebrandt International, a premier consulting firm generally to larger law firms and their managers. The program and its professors—in particular, Hildebrandt consultants Jim Jones and Carl Leonard, who both managed some of the nation's megafirms for about a decade[3]—provided great insight into the law firm operations. Their insights helped lift away the hood so that I could see how law firms' engines run. The George Washington University program also taught me a language to describe and a framework to understand law firm reality. Often, the best parts of this book reflect the lessons that I learned at the George Washington University program.

Third, in August 2007, I joined the *Lawyers for the Profession®* practice at Hinshaw & Culbertson, LLP. At Hinshaw, I focus my practice almost exclusively on advising lawyers, accountants, and their firms on issues including ethics, operations, and risk management. Through this focused practice, including discussions with firms and their management, I have the opportunity to observe and learn about how numerous law firms operate.

Finally, I have become something of a law practice management junkie. This habit manifests itself even through my pleasure readings, which include books on the history and development of many law firms, law firm management blogs, and countless articles on law firm marketing, management, and practice. My interest in law practice management has also led me to become involved in the American Bar Association's Law Practice Management Section,

---

[3]Jim Jones was Managing Partner of D.C.-based firm Arnold & Porter from 1986–95. Carl Leonard was Chairman of San Francisco-based Morrison & Foerster from 1984–93.

where I now serve on the Section's Council. Many of my friends are lawyers or people who advise lawyers. When we get together, one of the first things I usually want to learn is how the firms they know best operate.

Each of these sources has shaped parts of this book. Hopefully, they will combine to offer you an interesting, academic yet reality-grounded understanding of law firms and their operations. Hopefully, my experiences will also help you understand and navigate your opportunities so that you can find the right place, the firm, practice, and lifestyle that will provide you with happiness and job satisfaction.

Finally, many consider the 2008 economic downturn an event that has disrupted and may permanently change the private practice of law in the United States. The long-lasting impact of this downturn, as well as from concurrent technological advancement and globalization, remain uncertain. This book sometimes uses pre-downturn information to avoid over-emphasis of what may be a temporary situation, but also provides discussion and insight in case the 2008 downturn does have long-term impact on the legal profession.

Supplemental Resources

This book is designed to be used to teach those who will work with or at law firms. Support materials—including additional materials on topics addressed in this book as well as the Exercises it contains, presentation materials, and examples of many law firm documents—are available at **www.DowneyonLawPractice.com**.

1 Who and What Is a Law Firm?

It takes very little to make a law firm. For purposes of this book, a law firm consists of one or more lawyers who share some or all of the following: office space, clients, expenses, and revenues.

Prior to the start of the Twentieth Century, this basic description by itself largely captured the reality of most law firms. Most law firms were very small, effectively just office-sharing arrangements. Young lawyers typically arrived as apprentices. They studied and learned under a senior lawyer, and helped that senior lawyer with cases. Once the apprentice was prepared to handle his (or, rarely, her) own cases, the apprentice generally left and established a separate practice.

Sometimes a senior lawyer also developed too much work for one lawyer to handle, and asked an apprentice or former apprentice to help handle some of the work. Or sometimes an experienced lawyer shared office space with another experienced lawyer, and—while likely not working together much on matters—these lawyers might have divided up work.

Perhaps one handled all the transactional work, the other litigation, or they helped each other cover proceedings and the like. These two models became the first multi-lawyer firms.

In the early part of the Twentieth Century, the New York firm that became Cravath, Swain & Moore decided to break somewhat from the traditional model and start what is now known as the "Cravath system."[4] In the Cravath system, young lawyers are recruited to join the firm right out of law school. These young lawyers are then expected not to develop their own clients, but to work on matters for firm clients. After some period of years, some of these lawyers are invited to join the partnership and to assume an ownership interest in the firm. Others leave the firm, generally to take on other legal jobs (in-house counsel, government positions, and the like), non-legal positions, or to join another firm or open their own firms. Firms operating using a version of the Cravath system tend to be "up-or-out" system: a junior lawyer is promoted to partnership or is expected—and might be forced—to leave the firm.

As the Twentieth Century progressed, the largest firms in the country grew rapidly in size and sophistication. In the early 1900s, few firms had more than a handful of lawyers. As of 2007, the largest American-based law firm has almost 3,800 lawyers[5] More than 250 firms, meanwhile, have at least 170 lawyers.[6] Twelve American-based law firms have gross revenues in excess of $1 billion.[7]

Further, law firms employ hundreds of nonlawyer staff. These staff include secretaries, paralegals, filing clerks, runners, and others, who are performing jobs traditionally performed by law firm staff.

As law firms have grown and the legal profession has matured, firms have also become more sophisticated in their operations. Once, lawyers were solely responsible for marketing their practice, running the firm and supervising staff, and overseeing

---

[4]Milton Reagan, *Eat What You Kill* 20 (2004).

[5]National Law Journal, *The 2008 NLJ 250, available at* **http://www.law.com/jsp/nlj/PubArticleNLJ.jsp?id=1202425778391** (reporting DLA Piper has 3785 lawyers).

[6]*Id.*

[7]American Lawyer: *The Am Law 2008: Two Firms Pass the $2 Billion Mark, available at* **http://www.law.com/jsp/tal/PubArticleTAL.jsp?&id=1208947716661**.

completion of client work. But handling firm management became too time-consuming for lawyers, or lawyers decided it made sense to have a non-lawyer assist in certain capacities. Initially, some firms asked staff to assume additional or more specialized roles. A particularly able or skilled secretary or paralegal might assume responsibility for some marketing, or for managing information technology and staff.

By the latter portions of the Twentieth Century, the largest and most sophisticated firms retained specialized professionals to manage the firm and to handle various administrative capacities. A person with business or management expertise might be asked to become firm administrator, a trained accountant might be asked to take over the bookkeeping or chief financial officer role, and trained marketing staff might be asked to handle marketing functions.

Today, many firms have a managing director or chief operating officer, frequently a well-credentialed professional. Firms also hire marketing and human resources specialists to handle marketing and human resource tasks. Some firms employ literally scores of marketing personnel. They have people to write computer programs, manage information systems, data, and files, and even prepare electronic documents for production or electronic exhibits for trial. Also, the current trend in law firm management is for a law firm to identify the limited portion of the market for legal services it wants to serve, and then to arrange its resources to best serve that market. For many firms, this means stripping the resources from, and possibly even shedding away, practices that do not fit the firm's intended focus.

This overview should not be read to suggest that all firms are similar, or that all larger firms today have many lawyers and professional staff handling personnel, administration, finance, and information technology, or that they are narrowing their focuses. Rather, most lawyers still practice at firms with two or fewer lawyers. (In 2006, the ABA reported that 47 percent of lawyers in private practice were sole practitioners.)[8] Some markets, even

[8]American Bar Association, *Lawyer Demographics, available at* **http://www.abanet.org/marketresearch/lawyer_demographics_2006.pdf**.

some significant cities, may have only a handful of firms with more than a dozen lawyers. The exact traits of these firms vary, but many continue to use a combination of the lawyers, legal secretaries, and paralegals to handle all or virtually all aspects of the practice of law and the operation of the law firm. Many firms also handle virtually any legal work that walks in the door and that appears likely to pay.

Moreover, while this summary initial describes the typical growth of a standard, corporate-client focused firm, many firms today have a much more limited practice. A plaintiffs' firm, for example, may consist only of a couple of partners who receive help from some shared associates, paralegals, and legal secretaries. Another firm, particularly one that relies heavily on relatively small collection matters or bankruptcies, may have only a few attorneys, but rely on a great number of paralegals and legal assistants who help handle such smaller cases quickly and efficiently. A third firm may provide trust and estate services only to very high net worth individuals, and employ only very experienced lawyers as well as nonlawyers who possess appropriate skills and expertise—such as accounting or investing expertise—needed by such clients. A firm may even have most of its lawyers work from their homes, or use lawyers based in foreign countries. Few commonalities exist anymore among law firms—if they ever did. When considering or joining a firm, you should identify and assess how the features more unique to that firm are likely to coincide with your vision of your life and expected practice.

Virtual Law Firms

2

In addition to more traditional arrangements, virtual law firms are becoming more common. In a virtual law firm, normally a group of lawyers who have a common practice form a "firm" although they do not share a common space. To purists, a virtual law firm must use the Internet to provide legal services to clients. Many "virtual law firms" fail this requirement. Instead, many "virtual law firms" are mainly a joint marketing arrangement, and may also include a sharing of client information, collaborative efforts, and the like. Often such virtual firms also share significant computer linkage, so that the lawyers can interact freely although scattered somewhat across the country.

The Pittsburgh-based Delta Law Group, for example, reportedly has two partners that hold initial, face-to-face meetings with most new clients. After that initial meeting, most attorney-client communications are conducted through the law firm's interactive website. The attorneys who work on the clients' matters, meanwhile, are generally not the partner with whom the client initially met. Rather, the firm relies on specialists scattered throughout the Pittsburgh area.[9]

Another virtual firm, XDL Group, consists of nine lawyers who focus their practice on intellectual property (copyright, patent, and trade secret) litigation. The nine lawyers are located throughout the United States, and perceive themselves as the equivalent of a large firm's IP litigation assets (an IP litigator in several major IP litigation markets) with the overhead of a small firm.[10]

Sometimes, the term "virtual law firm" is also used to refer to a lawyer who works from home, communicates with clients primarily by Internet and telephone, and holds meetings at a client's office or rented meeting space. Some such firms even handle virtually all client intake over the Internet. Many of these lawyers are in reality sole practitioners who use technology to operate from home without rented office space.

[9]*See* Joyce Gannon, *Local law firm goes 'virtual': Delta one of handful that tries to conduct most of its business online*, Pittsburgh Post-Gazette (Jan. 18, 2008), *available at* **http://www.post-gazette.com/pg/08018/850124-28.stm?cmpid=business.xml#**.

[10]Larry Bodine, *Virtual Law Firm Unites Lawyers from 5 Law Firms*, Legal Marketing Technology (Aug. 2, 2007), *available at* **http://www.lawmarketing.com/pages/articles.asp?Action=Article&ArticleID=664**.

3 Office-Sharing Arrangements

In addition to law firms, a group of lawyers or law firms may share office space while not formally associating as a firm. Such office-sharing lawyers may literally share space with little other interaction. Perhaps each lawyer has his or her own office and secretarial space, and they share rent and use of some common areas like a conference, copying, or break room. Other times, the lawyers interact more: they may work together on matters or otherwise share client responsibilities. Normally, an office sharing arrangement can be identified by the fact that several lawyers practicing under different practice (firm) names share a common telephone line, which is answered "law offices."

The most common office-sharing arrangements involve lawyers (or small groups of lawyers) who operate law practices separate from the practices of their suite mates. These lawyers intend to operate and generally do operate as separate legal entities and law practices.

Lawyers participating in such arrangements must be careful, however, for certain types of conduct may cause the lawyers in an office-sharing arrangement to be considered members of a firm for legal or ethical purposes. Whether such an entity will be treated as a "firm" may depend upon why the issue is being considered. For business purposes, often the existence of a general partnership will turn on how the lawyers represent their relationship and how they operate the office. For example, a group of lawyers that closely shares revenues and expenses may be deemed a general partnership.[11]

Even if business operations are kept separate, a group of lawyers may be deemed a "firm" for ethics or malpractice reasons. Such determinations may focus on factors discussed above, but often turn on client expectations and the handling of client information. Normally a group of lawyers will be deemed a firm for purposes of the ethics rules (*e.g.*, the imputation of conflicts) if the lawyers (a) share client confidential information or (b) hold themselves out as a firm.[12] This may result in shared liability for attorneys who, despite separate practices, have chosen to operate in a manner that a client would perceive is a single firm.

Note that the line between an office-sharing arrangement and a law firm may be quite thin. Some law firms have compensation and other systems that result in lawyers sharing little more than office space and a firm name. Lawyers at such "law firms" develop their own practice—often with little overlap in expertise or clients—and practice with little regard for the rest of the firm. Such law firms may even divide expenses and cover salaries based upon how much they use staff or resources, much like office-sharing arrangements do. At these law firms, which are effectively a confederation of sole practitioners operating under a single firm name, the "managing partner" may serve only to make sure that common bills are paid, and to coordinate shared staff—such as a receptionist or possibly junior lawyers and paralegals.

---

[11]A general partnership may exist without formal documentation. It should not be confused with a limited partnership, which can only exist if certain formation documents are filed with a designated state regulator.

[12]*See, e.g.*, *Estate of Holmes v. Ludeman*, No. L-00-1294, 2001 WL 1198638 (Ohio App. Ct. Oct. 5, 2001).

Whether a group of lawyers are a law firm or individual practitioners can have significant impact on legal, ethical, and other liability. While this book will address risks for a firm later, lawyers who intend to share an office suite but otherwise operate separately should be careful that they do not inadvertently incur other legal or ethical risks by representing that or acting like they are members of a single firm.

Referral Arrangements Outside Law Firms

4

In addition to law firms and office-sharing arrangements, lawyers often refer matters to lawyers outside their own law firms. Three sets of circumstances account for most such referrals. First, many referrals occur because the matter is outside the jurisdiction where the lawyer first approached about the matter is licensed. For example, a client contacts a lawyer who has represented them in Baltimore and asks the lawyer if they can recommend a lawyer to handle a matter in Cleveland.

Second, referrals frequently occur because a lawyer cannot or does not handle the type of matter, or believes another lawyer may handle the matter better (or may be more willing to deal with the client). For example, a corporate transactional lawyer may refer a potential divorce case to a divorce lawyer because the transactional lawyer does not handle or want to handle the divorce, or the corporate lawyer may refer a patent matter to a patent lawyer because the corporate lawyer is not licensed to appear before the United States Patent and Trade Office. An additional example is one when a lawyer who handles a particular type of case, for example personal injury cases, refers a particularly complex or major matter to a personal injury lawyer more willing or able to take on and finance such a large and expensive case.

Third, some law firms refer work to other firms as a means of sharing the revenues generated. Law firms may advertise heavily on television and radio, using the advertisements to attract a large number of potential clients. These firms then refer all or a portion of the potential matters to other firms.

Many lawyers receive a large portion of their business on referral from other lawyers. Such referrals are also generally permitted under the ABA Model Rules of Professional Conduct and the ethics rules of the various states. In fact, the rule on competency encourages such referrals where the initial lawyer cannot provide competent representation.[13]

Sometimes the lawyer referring the matter will seek to share in the fees generated by the matter. Ethics rules for most jurisdictions impose limits on when lawyers who are not members of the same firm may share a fee and what requirements must be met for such fee-sharing arrangements to be valid. Model Rule 1.5(e), for example, allows lawyers not within a firm to share fees only when (a) the client agrees in writing to the fee-sharing arrangement and (b) either the fee-sharing arrangement is based on the proportion of work the lawyers provide or both lawyers agree to be responsible for the entire matter.[14]

Note, however, that while these limitations apply when lawyers are sharing offices, the limitations on referring work and fees do not apply when a lawyer refers work to other lawyers within the same firm. Generally, a lawyer may bring a new matter to the firm, have other lawyers work on the matter, and share in the fee without any client approval or formalization of the fee-shar-

[13] *See* ABA Model Rule 1.1 cmt [1].

[14] *See* generally ABA Model Rule 1.5(e). That many jurisdictions allow non-proportional sharing of fees only when both lawyers agree to be responsible for the entire case often causes firms to decline to share fees. A lawyer who first learns of a matter, but who expects to do no work on the matter, may be reluctant to assume potential liability for the entire representation.

ing arrangement. Why this discrepancy? Some believe it reflects a prejudice toward larger firms. Others believe the discrepancy is more an effort to look out for the client: in a law firm, the firm—and likely the lawyer who originates the matter—will retain responsibility for the entire matter and have at least some oversight over the representation, regardless of who at the firm works on the matter.

Referral arrangements may result in a network of law firms. But the ethics rules create limitations on such a referral network. Normally lawyers not within a firm may not enter an exclusive referral arrangement. Instead, each lawyer must remain free to exercise his or her professional judgment and refer the potential client to another lawyer that the lawyer referring the case believes will provide competent representation.

The Form of a Law Firm

5

Most law firms are (at least, de facto) a type of partnership: the partners in the firm share in the management and profits or losses of the firm. To limit liability, however, many firms also adopt some form of limited liability entity. Court rules or statutes generally do not permit law firms to operate as corporations. After Illinois changed its rules to allow lawyers to form limited liability companies and partnerships in 2003, however, every state now allows lawyers to operate in some limited liability form, such as a limited liability company, limited partnership, or professional corporation.

The variations between such forms, which primarily relate to governance, structure and tax treatment, do not matter a great deal for purposes of this book. Instead, each of these forms has several common features worth emphasizing. First, each allows multiple persons to own a portion of the entity. The exact title for such owners varies by entity type—limited partnerships have partners, limited liability companies have members, and professional corporations have shareholders. As is common, this book often uses "partners" to refer to owners regardless of their actual title. Second, each of these entities ordinarily has a governing document or agreement that establishes the rights and responsibilities of these owners. This document, which is a partnership agreement, operating agreement, or bylaws (for a limited liability company or professional corporation, respectively) will normally establish the name of the entity, its purposes, how it is managed and operates, how an owner can be added or removed, and the like. The agreement normally contains provisions related to the formation and dissolution of the firm and how the firm will be managed. The partnership or operating agreement also normally discusses how people become owners, how owners are compensated, and what happens when they cease to be owners. All these issues are addressed later in this book. Partnership or similar agreements vary in length from a handful of pages to 40 pages or, in some circumstances, many more.

A final, somewhat curious, note: many law firms, even firms that include corporate transactional lawyers, do not have a partnership or operating agreements. The absence of such a document may impair the ability of the firm to claim limited liability. More common problems relate to lack of clarity on requirements when a lawyer wants to leave the firm, or the firm wants to or is forced to dissolve.

Law Firm Governance

6

Most American law firms are governed on day-to-day issues by up to four groups of people: (1) the entire (equity)[15] partnership; (2) a management committee made up of equity partners; (3) a managing or administrative partner or partners, who are always or almost always equity partners; and (4) nonlawyer administrative staff, usually led by a firm administrator or (for larger firms) a chief operating officer overseen by a lawyer or group of lawyers. In addition, firms often delegate certain responsibilities to committees, which frequently include associate development and compensation, diversity, marketing, partner compensation, recruiting, and technology committees, plus a wide variety of other potential committees.

In many firms, particularly smaller firms, the entire partnership is likely to have an active role in firm management. But even at smaller firms, the lawyers often leave day-to-day operations, such as supervision of nonlawyer staff, supplies, technology, and

[15]The difference between equity and other parties is explained in Chapter 9.

financial activities (billing, collections, and paying bills), to a firm administrator.

Larger firms tend to delegate more control to a managing partner or management committee. Such delegation generally occurs through the partnership or operating agreement, which also likely reserves certain decisions for the partners. Decisions that commonly require vote of the firm's partners include:

- Admitting new partners
- Changing the status of or terminating a partner
- Changing the firm's name
- Amending the partnership or operating agreement
- Opening or closing an office
- Selecting the managing partner and management committee
- Approving partner compensation and the firm's budget

Some firms delegate even some of these decisions to the management committee or other group. Litigation between Chicago-based firm Sidley Austin Brown & Wood and the Equal Employment Opportunity Commission (EEOC) over demotion of 32 equity partners, for example, revealed that in the 1980s and 1990s the firm's partners had little control over the firm. Instead, almost all decisions were delegated to the firm's self-perpetuating Executive Committee. The Seventh Circuit described the relative power of partners and the Executive Committee as follows:

> Partners who are not members of the [executive] committee have some powers delegated to them by it with respect to the hiring, firing, promotion, and compensation of their subordinates, but so far as their own status is concerned they are at the committee's mercy. It can fire them, promote them, demote them . . . , raise their pay, lower their pay, and so forth. The only firm-wide issue on which all partners have voted in the last quarter century was [a] merger . . . and that vote took place after the EEOC began its investigation. Each of the 32 partners at the time of their demotion by the executive committee had a capital account with the firm, averaging about $ 400,000. Under the firm's rules, each was liable for the firm's liabilities in proportion to his capital in the firm. Their income, however, was determined by the number

> of percentage points of the firm's overall profits that the executive committee assigned to each of them. Each served on one or more of the firm's committees, but all these committees are subject to control by the executive committee.[16]

In some instances, in fact, a firm may authorize a managing partner unilaterally to hire or fire even an equity partner.[17]

This consolidation of control is not universal. Even some large firms continue to have the full partnership exert considerable control over the firm's operations. One of England's top—or "Magic Circle"—firms, Slaughter and May, makes almost all decisions through a vote of the firm's 126 equity partners.[18] Similarly, at Houston-based Susman Godfrey, firing a partner requires agreement from 75 percent of the partnership.[19]

Managing Partners

Most law firms assign primary responsibility for day-to-day management decisions to one managing partner, or a small number of such partners. These partners normally have responsibility for su-

---

[16]EEOC v. Sidley Austin Brown & Wood, 315 F.3d 696 (7th Cir. 2002). In 2002, the Seventh Circuit held that the EEOC could sue Sidley Austin for discrimination after the firm demoted 32 equity partners to non-equity status, although the anti-discrimination law protected only employees and not owners. The Seventh Circuit explained its conclusion that the demoted partners were protected under federal anti-discrimination laws in part by emphasizing that, although the 32 demoted lawyers were equity partners, all equity partners at the firm were at the mercy of the firm's thirty-six member, self-perpetuating Executive Committee. *See id.* Sidley Austin ultimately settled the discrimination suit by agreeing to pay $27.5 million. *See* Anthony Lin, *Sidley Austin Settles Age Bias Suit; No Determination of Merits*, N.Y. Law Journal (Oct. 8, 2007).

[17]Nate Raymond, *One-Man Firing Machine*, AmLaw Daily (June 9, 2008) (identifying Kasowitz, Benson Torres & Friedman and Bartlit Beck Herman Palenchar & Scott as two firms where the managing partner has sole control over hiring and firing of equity partners).

[18]Richard Lloyd, *Slaughter and May Names Saul New Senior Partner*, The American Lawyer (Jan. 22, 2008), *available at* **http://www.law.com/jsp/article.jsp?id=1200650735840**.

[19]Nate Raymond, *One-Man Firing Machine*, AmLaw Daily (June 9, 2008).

pervising the firm administrator, as well as handling whatever daily operations are not assigned to the administrator. Such partners may also have responsibility for coordinating pursuit of the firm's long-range plan.

Where short and long-term operations are divided, the short-term operations are sometimes assigned to one partner, normally called the "managing" or "administrative" partner. The longer-term responsibilities may be assigned to another partner, sometimes referred to as the firm's chair or president or, if the day-to-day manager does not use the title, the "managing" partner. Alternatively, the "chair" or "president" position may be a largely symbolic designation, likely given to a major rainmaker to recognize his or her importance to the firm, while the other administrative leader has responsibility for both short- and long-range issues.

Firms have very different rules regarding how managing attorneys are selected and how long managing attorneys can serve. Some firms provide that all equity partners elect the management committee, and then the management committee selects the managing partner(s). At other firms, the entire (equity) partnership selects the managing attorneys. At still other firms, a self-perpetuating management committee not only picks its own members but also selects the partner or partners who will run the firm.

Regarding term of service, sometimes managing attorneys may serve for a limited number of terms, each of a limited duration. At other firms, the managing attorney may remain in control for several decades, either through consistent reappointment, or because the firm only selects a managing partner when the incumbent managing partner wants to resign.[20]

Participation in law firm management is quite different from serving as the chairman or chief executive officer of a corporation. Corporate leaders are often chosen from outside the company, are

---

[20]The West Virginia-based Steptoe & Johnson PLLC, for example, had a single lawyer serve as chair and chief executive officer for more than 30 years. That lawyer, Robert M. Steptoe, Jr. stepped down as CEO in 2008, but continued to serve as the firm's chairman and to practice labor and employment and civil litigation at the firm. *See* Peter Page, *BigLaw Firm Selects First Female CEO*, National Law Journal (Jan. 18, 2008). The West Virginia-based firm is one of two firms that use the Steptoe & Johnson name.

given considerable authority in running the company, and leave the company when their term as leader ends.

Law firm managing attorneys, however, almost always rise from the ranks to join management of the firm. Despite their management status, these managing attorneys often lack much control over the firm and other partners because of the partnership and management structure, and the importance of equity partners as the developers, producers, and managers of client work. Often the managing attorneys answer to the equity partners and possess very little power to compel equity partners—particularly major rainmakers—to do anything against their will. Moreover, when a lawyer's service in management ends, the managing attorney normally continues to practice as an equity partner and practicing lawyer.

Managing attorneys of a law firm often must answer to all equity partners at the firm, including their close professional friends as well as one or more equity partners who at some point were themselves managing partners. The managing attorneys must also try to maintain their clients and practice skills so that one day they can resume their role as an equity partner.

These differences sometimes make the managing partner position somewhat undesirable, such that a candidate must be coaxed into taking the role. But many lawyers will savor the position because they believe a management position will help them run the show, or that participation in the management of the firm—or at least holding a title that suggests participation in such management—will help the lawyer develop more business.

Problems in Law Firm Governance

Law firms frequently suffer from governance problems. Leaders generally lack leadership training and sometimes leadership skills, they are often selected for the wrong reasons, and the structure of law firms makes leading a firm difficult.

While many companies are led by people with management degrees, and many companies invest significant time, money, and other resources in teaching managers how to lead, most law firms have traditionally devoted very few resources to developing leaders. Normally a managing attorney has no management training, and likely limited management experience, when that person is selected as a managing attorney. The managing attorney then spends little time trying to learn how to lead a law firm. Rather, managing attorneys often devote their education time to learning more about the present condition of the firm or updating themselves on their substantive area of legal practice.

Law firms also struggle because persons chosen to lead law firms generally are not chosen because of their leadership skills. Many firms choose leaders based upon the lawyers' acumen in practicing law or developing business, not in leading individuals. A Midwestern firm with about two dozen attorneys, for example, sets compensation based upon fees collected and fees originated, and then names its top grossing partner the managing partner for the upcoming year—and the next handful of highest grossing partners to the remaining slots on the management committee. Such systems reward performance, and insure those who are generating the most for the firm also have a direct say in how the firm is run. But they ignore that often people who excel in generating business or practicing law may not have the skills, personality, or interest necessary to the firm well.

Leadership decisions are also often very political, resulting in poor selections and sometimes significant political problems. While some lawyers (even some good potential leaders) see management as an unwanted and unrewarded headache, others see firm management as a prize to win or a way to keep others from meddling in their practices. Sometimes powerful lawyers—generally powerful rainmakers—insist that they or their disciples receive leadership positions. Often, this results in the selection of law firm leaders who do not want to devote their time to leading the firm, or who are intentionally kept weak.

Often firm management also lacks the power to select other leaders, and the ability to punish or reward other leaders at the firm. At a company, often the board of directors selects the top manager, who then builds his or her team to manage the rest of the entity. At most law firms, however, partners select—from amongst themselves—the persons who will lead the firm, and also the persons who will lead subdivisions of the firm (such as practice group leaders). This often prevents a managing lawyer from exercising authority over the other partners, and even over the leaders of various subsections. Instead of the partners being accountable to practice group leaders, and practice group leaders being accountable to firm management, the management and practice group leaders may instead be accountable to the partners—even if there are hundreds of partners. Such disjointed accountability generally makes it difficult for a firm leader to exercise much control within a firm—a trait many partners may actually like, for many lawyers dislike or distrust management.

Such structural weaknesses make it difficult to control the most powerful or successful lawyers. Normally companies have specific people, plants, and equipment that are developed and focused to carry out different tasks. A company may have managers, human resources, sales, and production personnel. Also, a company often has separate sales offices, customer service centers, and production facilities. A traditional law firm, however, has its partners, who are expected to run the firm, develop new clients and matters, and also produce the most significant or valuable legal work for clients. A partner who generates significant revenue for the firm may insist upon a serving in a particular management role, or may choose to ignore firm management. The firm must then decide whether to accede to this partner's desires, recognizing that a failure to do so may cause the lawyer to leave and take his or her clients with him. Professional regulations make such risks quite real, for generally (a) lawyers may not offer or enter non-compete agreements under ABA Model Rule 5.6, and (b) clients may change law firms, or fire a law firm to follow a favorite lawyer to a new firm, at any time.

Finally, lawyers chosen to lead firms or practice groups are frequently compensated not for their performance as managers, but for performance as lawyers—in other words, for developing and serving clients. Many firms give partners little or no credit for the time they spend managing the firm or addressing firm problems. Coupled with general lack of authority, training, and interest, this lack of compensation often ensures that lawyers spend little time and effort on firm management issues.

Recent Improvements in Law Firm Governance

Recently, some firms have begun to make changes to address such issues. Some firms—particularly large firms—have sought formal leadership training for their current and future lawyer managers. Programs such as DLA Piper's program at Harvard Business School, Reed Smith University through the Wharton Business School of the University of Pennsylvania, and Seyfarth Shaw's partner management training at Northwestern University's Kellogg School of Management, or the arrangement Buchanon Ingersoll has made with law firm consulting firm Altman Weil, now provide formal management and leadership training for the future leaders of law firms.[21] A 2008 study indicates, however, that only about 20 percent of large law firms have leadership development programs.[22] Most smaller firms have only informal training, if anything.

Also, some firms are beginning to let firm leaders select, direct, and evaluate their own leadership team. They are also trying to teach lawyers that management requires particular skills, and should not simply be a reward for performance in some other aspect of lawyering. Finally, some law firms are altering their compensation systems to compensate managers for time spent managing, and to reward managers for their successes in managing the firm.

---

[21]Leigh Jones, *Back to School for Partners*, National Law Journal (July 20, 2005); Douglas B. Richardson & Douglas P. Coopersmith, *Management: Learning to Lead*, American Lawyer (July 1, 2008).

[22]Douglas B. Richardson & Douglas P. Coopersmith, *Management: Learning to Lead*, American Lawyer (July 1, 2008).

7 The Career Lattice for Larger-Firm Lawyers

Today many large law firms continue to employ a hiring and promotion process modeled on the so-called Cravath system.[23] These firms hire new attorneys straight from law school, often using law student summer associate programs to identify, court, and vet candidates. They have these new lawyers work on matters for firm clients for several years. Often, the new lawyers are discouraged—or at least not encouraged—to develop their own clients during this period.

After the new lawyer has been at the firm several years, generally at least five and sometimes more than ten years, the partnership of the law firm decides (elects) whether to ask that lawyer to join partnership. If the lawyer is elected, he or she may remain at the law firm as a partner. If a lawyer is not elected, or declines the partnership offer, the lawyer may be handled in a

---

[23]The 2008 economic downturn has raised questions whether most larger firms will continue to use a version of the Cravath system. As of publication, firms have decreased the number of summer associates and new lawyers they are hiring, but most larger firms continue to use a version of the Cravath system.

number of ways. At a minority of larger firms (and by larger here I mean a law firm with ten or more lawyers), the lawyer not elected to partnership is expected to or required to leave the firm. These firms, which include both small firms as well as some of the country's most profitable large firms, use an "up-or-out" system.

At most such larger lawyer firms, however, a lawyer who does not become a partner has other options. At these firms, generally referred to as "up-or-over" firms, a lawyer not joining the partnership may receive reconsideration for partnership at a later time, or move off the partnership track but remain at the firm as a senior lawyer.

Once a lawyer achieves equity partner, many—likely most—lawyers do not advance further in the profession. They may become leaders in their practice group or firm, but as suggested above such positions are not necessarily promotions. Also, an equity partner may obtain more shares in the firm, and thus more political power and more compensation, as the equity partner's practice develops. But such an increase in shares normally depends more upon how much business the lawyer develops than longevity at the firm or other factors.

In addition to promotions at a firm, many lawyers today change firms during their careers. These moving lawyers, generically referred to as "laterals," might have been partners or associates at the firm they left, and they may be promoted or demoted as a result of their move. Often an associate nearing consideration for partnership at a firm who changes firms will need to wait a few years before being considered for partnership at the new firm. Also, a lawyer may be promoted when moving to a firm with a lower financial or other threshold for partnership, or include promotion to partnership or consideration for partnership as a condition for accepting a lateral move.

The following is a sample lawyer promotion schedule:

Years post law-school graduation	Title
1–3	Junior associate
4–6	Senior associate
6–7+	Senior attorney
If elected to partnership	
6–12+	Non-equity partner

If elected to equity partnership	
6–40+	Equity partner
Mandatory retirement	
40+	Senior counsel

The following chapters will explain—and expand upon—these various categories. Before doing so, however, it is worth noting this schedule is far too simplified.

First, law firms often do not use all the titles on the schedule. Some firms still have only partners, or partners and associates. Others have only one level of associate or one level of partner. Many also do not use "senior attorney" as a step on the promotion ladder; instead, they use the term to designate a lawyer passed over for partnership but who remains in the firm in a senior capacity. Such variations exist at all sizes and types of firms.

Second, the number of years from graduation is a gross oversimplification. Some firms, particularly smaller firms but also some larger firms, consider a lawyer for partnership far faster than eight years. Eight years is an approximation of common tracks to the lower tier of partnership, where a firm has a lower tier. Particularly at a very small firm, a new lawyer may become a partner almost immediately, particularly if that lawyer is able to develop or manage a substantial amount of business.

Additionally, as discussed above, lateral attorneys may move up or down the career ladder faster because of their lateral move. For example, firms often want to have some time to know a younger lawyer before considering that lawyer for partnership. Therefore, a more senior associate—for example, a sixth-year attorney—may have to wait a year or two longer than ordinary to be considered for partnership. In another example, a particularly appealing, more senior associate may change firms based on a commitment that the firm will elect or consider electing the lawyer a partner in a shorter period of time. Thus, promotion may be more of a lattice than a ladder.

Despite such complexities, the following are offered as summaries of the various rungs on lawyers' career ladders.

Non-Partner Lawyers

8

Associates (Including Junior and Senior Associates)

The most junior lawyers in a firm who (at least initially) are on partnership track[24] are referred to almost universally as "associates." Sometimes a firm will divide associates between "junior" and "senior" associates. Normally, these titles have limited purposes: to recognize the lawyer for tenure and ability, to justify charging a client more for the lawyer's services, and the like. Senior associates may also have a bit more involvement in firm management. In general, however, the "junior" and "senior" titles for associates provide few benefits or differences for those associates.

Associates are often the worker bees of the law firm. Normally they perform client work, and have fewer expectations and responsibilities for developing new business and participating in management of the firm. In light of such limited responsibilities, it can be

[24]Some firms have junior lawyers who are not on a partnership track. These lawyers, sometimes referred to as "staff attorneys," are described below in Chapter 10.

tempting for a lawyer to focus on the work and ignore the larger reality of the firm. As will be discussed in much greater detail in this book, however, a decision to ignore client development, firm responsibility, and the like may limit long-term the ability of a lawyer to develop himself or herself. This decision in turn may limit advancement at the firm. At some firms and in some instances, a partner may be in the position to hand off a successful practice or group of faithful clients to a loyal and capable junior lawyer. In many instances, however, a junior lawyer will need to be prepared to and ultimately take responsibility for his or her own career.

According to an Altman Weil survey, the median associate compensation in 2007 was $123,050.[25] But many law firm associates make more or less than this amount. As described in the compensation section below, some new associates receive salaries of $30,000 or so, while others receive salaries of $180,000 or more. Pay may also include an element or bonuses based upon performance, including for number of hours billed (or billed and collected), business originated, or for other particular activities. In general, the 2008 economic downturn has caused associate salaries to remain level or decline.

Senior Attorneys

The designations "senior attorney," "of counsel," and "special counsel" are sometimes used interchangeably by a firm. They are generally titles of recognition that the lawyer has been practicing longer than (most of) the associates at the firm. They also generally indicate the firm intends to bill the lawyer at a higher rate.

Lawyers earn the "senior attorney" designation through a variety of ways. At some firms, it is an intermediate step between the highest associate rank and the lowest tier of partnership. An attorney must pass through this rank on the way to partnership. At other firms, a "senior attorney" title may designate a senior lawyer who is not on the partnership track, either by choice or because the firm decided not to make that person a partner.

[25]*New Survey Provides Snapshot of Law Firm Economics Across U.S.* (Aug. 2, 2007).

Senior Counsel

The "senior counsel" title may simply be another alternative to "senior attorney." However, this book and some firms use it to designate an attorney who has (voluntarily or involuntarily) retired from or aged out of the partnership or joined the firm after a significant practice outside the firm and are not expected to move into partnership. Some firms also use the title "senior partner" to refer to such attorneys, although more often this is a designation for a major equity partner or rainmaker.

In approximately 2007, various groups, including the ABA, began calling on firms to end mandatory retirement policies.[26] Nevertheless, many law firms continue to have mandatory retirement ages. These provisions generally force equity partners to relinquish ownership and at some firms retire from the practice of law between the ages of 60 and 75.[27] Such policies are thought to allow younger partners to assume more significant roles both with clients and within the firm, and to allow the partnership to remain more vigorous in its leadership.[28] But the legality of some such arrangements has been in serious doubt since the Equal Employment Opportunity Commission (EEOC) brought an age-discrimina-

---

[26]Lisa van der Pool, *Law firm's 'gray ceilings' may be changing colors: Courts put a price on mandatory retirement*, Boston Business Journal (Feb. 1, 2008), contains a discussion of mandatory retirement policies, the ABA's call to end policies, and the decision by several large firms to terminate their mandatory retirement policy.

[27]*Id.*

[28]Sometimes the combination of mandatory retirement plus lateral partner movements can have interesting unintended consequences. In a 2008 *New York Lawyer* article, former Powell Goldstein partner David S. Baker discussed the transition of his long-time client, Atlanta's Northside Hospital, to a younger partner as preparation for Baker's mandatory retirement. The younger partner then left Powell Goldstein, taking the client with him. Baker asserted that "if he hadn't been required to retire from Powell Goldstein, Northside would 'absolutely' continue to be a client of the firm." Meredith Hobbs, *BigLaw Partner Rejects Mandatory Retirement, Jumps to Boutique Founded by Ex-Partners*, New York Lawyer (Mar. 12, 2008). Powell Goldstein's retirement policy, adopted in the 1970s, required semi-retirement at age 65 and full retirement prior to a lawyer's 71st birthday. After retirement, the partner could have an office at the firm, but would not have much work to do. *Id.*

tion claim against Sidley Austin. This suit, which is discussed above[29] and resulted in a $27.5 million settlement entered by Sidley Austin in October 2007, arose largely from a decision of the firm to de-equitize a group of senior equity partners.

After the Sidley Austin settlement was announced, the ABA took the position that law firms should abandon their mandatory retirement provisions. Some firms dropped mandatory retirement policies after the ABA made its recommendation in August 2007. Nationally, firms that have dropped such policies include Pillsbury Winthrop Shaw Pittman LLP and K&L Gates.

Lawyers who do not fully retire under such plans often become senior counsels at the firm. Some senior counsels maintain full, active practices. Some move into alternative activities, such as mediating cases, mentoring associates, or the like. Firms continue to find new opportunities and practices for senior counsels.

The "Of Counsel" Designation

The "of counsel" designation can have widely different meanings, even at a single firm.

There are at least four major uses for the "of counsel" designation. First, "of counsel" is used to describe a lawyer who is associated with a law firm, but not actually integrated into the firm. For example, a lawyer might be a partner in one firm but, due to an ongoing group of matters, the lawyer might also want to establish and publicize an ongoing relationship with a second firm. Or a lawyer may want to work part-time with the firm, perhaps while retaining a separate profession (as a law professor or something outside the practice of law). The term "of counsel" is used to describe these relationships.

Second, the term "of counsel" was and still is sometimes used to describe the relationship of two law firms working together, such as the relationship between local and national counsel.

---

[29] *See* Law Firm Governance, Chapter 6.

Third, "of counsel" is used as an alternative to "senior attorney" to describe a lawyer who is senior to the associates at the firm but not a partner. This might be someone who had joined the firm but is not of sufficient stature to become a non-equity partner or contract partner (discussed in the next section).

Fourth, "of counsel" is frequently used as an alternative to "senior counsel" to describe the senior lawyer, perhaps even a former equity partner, who due to age or years of practice or the like has decided to or is forced to reduce his or her workload, at least with regard to the management of the firm.

9 Partnership

As discussed earlier, often a lawyer will advance through one or several non-partner levels based upon longevity of practice. At some point, that lawyer likely will be considered for and possibly elected to partnership. Most law firms categorize partners in up to three ways. Most firms have a lower tier of "non-equity partners" and an upper tier of "equity partners." Some also have a third category called "contract partners."[30] Ordinarily a lawyer must be elected to partnership, and frequently a non-equity partner must also be elected or admitted to equity partnership. These promotions, particularly the move to equity partner, are often far more challenging than the promotions from junior associate to senior associate and the like. After all, a move from junior to senior associate normally has the primary impact of increasing the lawyer's billing rates. The move to equity partner, meanwhile, may not re-

[30]A 2006 Altman Weil survey found 85 percent of firms with more than 100 lawyers had two-tier partnerships. *See* Jim Cotterman, *What Does Non-Equity Really Mean?* (Nov. 15, 2007), *available at* **http://blog.altmanweil.com/**.

sult in an increase in billing rate, but it likely requires the firm's other equity partners to share the firm's profits with the new equity partner.[31]

In describing these lawyers, I have used the term "partner." This term suggests ownership, which, except as described below, is generally accurate. Depending upon the legal form of the law firm, it may be more appropriate for the owning lawyers to be called by a different title, for example:

Corporate Form	Owner Designation
Limited Liability Company (LLC)	Member
Limited Liability Partnership (LLP)	Partner
Professional Association (PA)	Shareholder
Professional Corporation (PC)	Shareholder

However, for simplicity, I will continue to use the term "partner" to refer to all such owners.

Many firms do not publicly distinguish between different types of partners. For example, everyone except partners at a firm may be unable to determine which partners are equity partners and which are non-equity partners. Also, when a firm announces partnership decisions, this announcement is normally made when a lawyer reaches the lowest tier of partnership, generally the non-equity position. A move from non-equity to equity partnership is often not announced outside the firm partnership itself. Thus, associates and staff—other than perhaps a firm administrator—may not know that a person has been elected an equity partner.

While this book discusses some general principles for partners and their powers, to a great extent the relationship of partners to the firm—including their ability to control the firm and right to receive payments from it—are governed by a contractual document such as a partnership agreement or (for a limited liabil-

[31]Sometimes a junior lawyer may be "guaranteed" partnership as an inducement to join a firm, stay with a firm, or the like. Courts are often very reluctant to treat such promises of partnership as enforceable. *See, e.g.*, *Hoeffner v. Orrick, Herrington & Sutcliffe*, 602694/05 (N.Y. Sup. Ct. Aug. 1, 2008).

ity company, for example) an operating agreement. This document was discussed earlier,[32] but references to it necessarily abound here.

Equity Partners

Equity partners—also called capital partners, shareholders, or members—are the lawyers who own voting shares of a firm. As discussed later, they may purchase these shares through capital contributions, either by helping establish the firm or by paying for their shares (generally by literally buying the shares or by earning them through their contribution to the firm and its revenues). As a consequence of their ownership in the firm, equity partners may vote to effect the operation of the firm, including whether the firm should merge or dissolve, and who should lead it. Sometimes, or at some firms, votes are weighted based upon the number of ownership shares a partner possesses.

At most law firms today, equity partners are the most powerful group of lawyers. They ordinarily dominate the management and compensation committees which run the firm and set partnership compensation respectively. Equity partners also ordinarily take a lead both in managing the firm and its resources and in supervising client work. As discussed in Chapter 6, equity partners commonly must vote to approve firm actions such as:

- Admitting new partners
- Changing the status of or terminating a partner
- Changing the firm's name or partnership agreement
- Opening or closing an office
- Selecting the managing partner and management committee
- Approving partner compensation and the firm's budget

Such votes may require approval from a majority of the equity partners, a supermajority of the equity partners, or a majority or

[32]*See* The Form of a Law Firm, Chapter 5.

supermajority of the ownership interests in the firm (which then give additional political power to those shareholders with the most shares).

Equity partners are also the lawyers with the most at stake in a firm: they share in the firm's profits during the good times, but also in losses in the bad times. Although equity partners often receive or have the right to take a monthly "draw," or portion of the profits they are likely to earn at the end of the year, their compensation is largely determined by what share of profits they receive at the end of the year. Thus, in a particularly lean year, there may be very little left for the equity partners to divide.

A lawyer normally becomes an equity partner because he or she controls or originates a significant amount of business. (This may be more than a million dollars of business at the largest and most affluent firms in New York City or other major coastal metropolitan areas, or several hundred thousand dollars of business in other firms). Often, a lawyer must practice at the firm for some time, even if a lateral from another firm, before becoming an equity partner. As noted above,[33] it is not unusual for a larger firm to require all non-partners to work for two or more years as a non-equity partner before that person becomes an equity partner. Further, some partners never become equity partners—although at some firms, failure to qualify for equity partnership within a period may result in the lawyer being asked to leave the firm.

As their name suggests, equity partners generally acquire equity in the firm. Often this capital contribution or "buy-in" process requires the lawyer to pay the firm $10,000s or even $100,000s to purchase shares. Normally, either every lawyer pays in the same amount, or a lawyer buys, either directly or by relinquishing income or earned profits to the firm, equity shares up to a certain cap, which is often based upon the lawyer's business and fees generated. The portion of income relinquished may be substantial: one article reports that at K&L Gates equity partners are expected to contribute 35 percent of their earnings as capitol to the firm.[34]

---

[33]*See* Career Lattice for Larger Firm Lawyers, Chapter 7.

[34]Leigh Jones, *The Price of Partnership Is Going Up,* National Law Journal (July 8, 2008).

Equity partners may accumulate significant capital in their firm capital account. The 32 lawyers who were demoted by Sidley Austin in the late 1990s, for example, had an average of $400,000 in capital invested in the firm.[35] Such investments may come through an initial buy-in, but often they are supplemented by a firm rule that requires a lawyer to retain a certain amount of money or a certain amount of compensation in their capital account. The firm can then use this money to pay firm expenses, such as capital expenditures or the like.

How do lawyers afford buy-in? Some law firms leave it to the lawyer to determine financing. But many firms either allow a lawyer to pay over time, or to borrow from the firm or from a financial institution with whom the firm has previously made arrangements. Thus, for some lawyers, making partnership may seem like a tempting time to move to a new house, but the lawyer may end up effectively with two mortgages—the new house, and also the expenses incurred in paying off the partnership buy-in. Moreover, at some firms an equity partner may experience a reduction in net income for the first few years of equity partnership because, while gross pay may increase, a new partner often assumes greater responsibility for taxes, insurance, and other benefits.

When an equity partner leaves a firm, the departing lawyer ordinarily has a right to recover the amount of capital or equity invested in the firm. But firms vary greatly on when they are required to return capital to a departing partner. Former intellectual property firm Fish & Neave, for example, had up to four years to repay partnership contributions.[36] Most firms must repay contributions sooner, generally within a few months or a year of an equity partner's departure.

Not all equity partners are equals. At many firms, equity partners do not own equal shares of equity in the firm. At some firms, the number of shares an equity partner owns may vary based upon some formula calculated on an annual or semi-annual basis. Some equity partners own more, and others less. Often the lawyer with more equity shares has more power at the firm, and also receives greater compensation. There may even be certain "gates"

---

[35]*EEOC v. Sidley Austin Brown & Wood*, 315 F.3d 696 (7th Cir. 2002).

[36]Leigh Jones, *The Price of Partnership Is Going Up*, New York Lawyer (July 8, 2008).

where an equity partner must meet certain requirements to move to a higher compensation tier; for example, there may be 15 levels of equity partners, but the top 3 are reserved only for those who pass a "gate" by demonstrating exceptional revenue-producing capabilities. Additional information on partner compensation is provided in Chapter 23.

Being an equity partner is often not easy. Equity partners must actually run the firm, a task for which most were not trained and for which few are well predisposed (most would prefer just to practice law, serve clients, make money, and be left alone). This burden is particularly great at smaller firms, which generally cannot afford to have lawyers only manage and not practice. Further, they are the one group of lawyers at a firm who do not really know their compensation at the beginning of the year: if the firm has a horrible year, associates may lose their bonuses but at least still receive their salaries. Equity partners have no such guarantee—and they are also the ones who will be left paying, for instance, malpractice judgments and government fines. Often equity partners also must provide personal guarantees for leases and the like.

Finally, the position of equity partner is not a safe one even at the nation's largest and most successful firms. Each year in its May issue, the *American Lawyer* publishes the *Am Law 100*, a list of the 100 largest and most profitable firms as ranked by their profits per equity partner.[37] Many perceive this as "the" list for large, national firms, the one by which they judge their relative prestige. Perhaps driven by this list, the largest firms have taken numerous steps to increase their profits per equity partner, including demoting or firing equity partners as well as increasing the requirements for equity partnership. In 2006, for example, 39 of these firms decreased or held steady their number of equity partners. Another 14 added fewer than 3 equity partners. Some firms have been steadily trimming equity partners: between 2004 and 2007, 25 percent of equity partners have departed from Cadwalader, Wickersham & Taft; 18 percent from Dechert; and 17 per-

[37] *The Am Law 100* list generally omits plaintiffs' firms and smaller firms, and focuses on larger firms that mainly represent companies.

cent from Morrison & Foerster.[38] As the *American Lawyer* summarized, "The new rules of partnership? Tenure is dead. Produce (at an attractive rate) or perish."[39]

A large firm's status on this list may also be subject to temporary circumstances. Although a profitable firm, Wiley Rein would not necessarily be one expected to grab the top spot on the *Am Law 100.* It achieved that spot in 2007, however, with profits per equity partner reportedly at $4.4 million but fueled in significant part by $200 million in fees the firm received from representing NTP in its patent litigation against BlackBerry manufacturer RIM.[40]

While the dollar figures may be different, similar problems impact equity partners at smaller firms. A firm may obtain fewer contingency fees in a year, or lose a key client, or have a key lawyer or group of lawyers depart. All these events can have a major impact on equity partner compensation.

Not all firms have multiple equity partners. In 2008, the 250-lawyer firm Dreier LLP made news when Marc Dreier, the sole equity partner at the firm, was arrested and charged with fraud. News coverage sometimes suggested that Dreier was unusual because it had only one equity partner. This is not the case. Drier was likely the largest law firm to have a single equity partner, but many smaller firms—particularly personal injury or other firms whose business development is driven largely by the personality and reputation of one large rainmaker—have only one equity partner.

Finally, in every United States jurisdiction except the District of Columbia, only lawyers may have ownership interests in a law firm.[41] This long-held principle has come under challenge of late, however, particularly after the Australian law firm Slater & Gordon became publicly traded in May 2007. Recent changes in English

---

[38]Aric Press and John O'Connor, *Lessons of the Am Law 100,* American Lawyer (May 1, 2007), *available at* **http://www.law.com/jsp/tal/PubArticleTAL.jsp?hubtype=Cover+Story&id=1177578266432.**

[39]*Id.*

[40]Peter Lattman, *Hot Off the Presses: the Am Law 100,* WSJ Law Blog (Apr. 30, 2007), *available at* **http://blogs.wsj.com/law/2007/04/30/hot-off-the-presses-the-amlaw-100/.**

[41]*See* ABA Model Rule 5.4(b) & (d).

law make it more likely that English firms will seek to encourage outside investment of capital through ownership. This is expected to increase pressure for American jurisdictions to allow nonlawyer ownership of law firms.

Non-Equity Partners

As their name suggests, non-equity partners differ from equity partners primarily because non-equity partners do not own equity in the law firm. Non-equity partnership may be an interim point between the ranks of non-partner and those of equity partners where a lawyer will stay approximately five years before being considered for advancement. In many firms, however, some lawyers may be promoted to non-equity partner but no further. Also, sometimes equity partners are demoted or stripped of their equity status, usually because of comparatively low business origination. This process is called *de-equitization*.

A 2006 survey of 58 managing partners at law firms with more than 100 lawyers reported the following information about non-equity partners:

- the largest group were promoted from associate but were deemed not yet ready to become equity partners
- next came lawyers promoted from associate but not expected to become equity partners
- next were laterals deemed not yet ready to become equity partners
- a final small group had been demoted from equity partnership

Several other reasons were also listed for non-equity partners, including equity partners on maternity or disability leave and those transitioning toward retirement.[42]

[42]Charles Toutant, *Most Tier Partners Still 'On Path' to Equity Status, Survey Finds,* N.J. Law Journal (May 25, 2006), *available at* **http://www.law.com/jsp/llf/PubArticleLLF.jsp?id=1148461531071&rss=llf.**

Prior to the 2008 economic downturn, the trend for firms was to increase significantly their use of non-equity partners. According to *Law Firm, Inc.*, equity partners at AmLaw 200 firms[43] increased 40 percent but non-equity partners increased 160 percent in the early 2000s.[44] The 2008 downturn may have slowed this process, however, because some firms are laying off non-equity partners instead of lower-paid (and likely more flexible) associates.

In most firms, the non-equity partner status allows a lawyer to become a "partner"—a title that helps in marketing a practice and in assuming control over client matters—and to enjoy some perks of partnership without the greatest rewards of partnership, control of the firm and a share of profits. Law firms may give non-equity partners larger offices and more support than non-partners. Non-equity partners may also be invited to participate in partnership meetings and to vote on certain matters, such as non-partner compensation.

Finally, it is important to note that at some firms "non-equity" partner is a misnomer. In such firms, a person selected to the lowest tier of partnership is expected to buy-in—pay for a portion of the capital. Such buy-ins can be quite expensive, usually substantially more than $10,000. Often lower-tier partners who end up acquiring shares have few or no voting rights. Also, often these lower-tier partners receive compensation that is set or substantially guaranteed, as through a contract or formula.

Contract Partners

In their most common form, contract partners are lateral partners who join a law firm, normally after having built a practice and portable book of business at a prior firm. They enter a "contract" with the new firm. This contract states what the contract partner must do to obtain certain levels of compensation. Thus, a partner

[43]The *American Lawyer* ranks large law firms by profits per equity partner. The AmLaw 200 would be the 200 firms ranked highest on this survey.

[44]*The Axman Cometh*, LawFirm, Inc. 11 (Dec. 2007).

may be required to generate $600,000 in fees through billable time, and originate at least $600,000 in business, in order to receive a certain level of compensation or a certain portion of the revenues they generate. The contract may also specify when the contract partner will be considered for admission to the firm as an equity partner. This period is usually about one to three years.

In many ways, a firm's contract partners are often quite similar to non-equity partners. Contract partners normally cannot and do not buy fully into the firm's ownership. They often have more limited powers to vote on major firm actions, partnership compensation, and the like. However, they are sometimes permitted to participate more in the management of the firm, and often have significantly greater stature than the typical non-equity partner. In fact, a partner who moves to another law firm without significant portable business will likely be required to serve for a period as a senior attorney/counsel or non-equity partner instead of becoming a contract or equity partner.

10 Temporary and Contract Attorneys

In addition to attorneys employed or fully associated with a firm, in recent years the legal profession has seen considerable growth in the use of temporary or contract attorneys. The distinguishing characteristic of such a lawyer is that he or she does not expect to work with the firm or on a matter forever. Often, they are hired through a temporary agency to handle a specific case or task, or to work for a specific period. Generally, they are treated as independent contractors, not employees of the law firm.

The terms "temporary" and "contract" attorney are often used interchangeably, but there are really two separate types of attorneys:

- First, those lawyers whom this text calls "temporary attorneys" are hired for a short period of time and operate largely outside the operations of the firm. These lawyers are often brought in to handle large, lawyer-intensive but temporary projects such as document reviews, business transaction due diligence, or the like. Sometimes temporary lawyers' work may resemble paralegal work, for the temporary lawyers may work for and under the direct supervision of a firm lawyer (often an associate, possibly one with far less experience than the temporary lawyer). In other instances, the temporary workers may operate somewhat more autonomously. Such autonomy normally results in the temporary lawyer being more akin to what this text calls a "contract attorney."

- Second, those lawyers whom this text calls "contract attorneys" are normally hired for a longer period of time. Such lawyers are often retained to handle a particular case or group of cases, and often serve as the main lawyer or one of the main lawyers on the specified group of matters. These lawyers may prepare pleadings or documents, handle depositions, virtually anything a firm lawyer would do, often with considerable independence. However, they are ordinarily treated and paid as independent contractors, not employees. They generally have no chance of advancement within the firm, and will end their relationship with the firm when their matters are completed.

Sometimes a lawyer hired to work with a firm has some characteristics of a contract and a temporary lawyer. For example, lawyers may be hired through a temporary agency to work on a particular document production, and work on that document production, for a single client and matter, for several years.

Note also that "contract lawyer" and "contract partner" as used in this book denote very different lawyer roles. A contract lawyer is a lawyer who normally will be at a firm for a limited time and who will generally not be considered for promotion within the firm. A contract partner, meanwhile, is normally a lawyer who is being paid according to a contract, but who is expected to become an equity partner at the firm and to remain at the firm long term.

11 Nonlawyers at Law Firms

In addition to lawyers, most law firms employ nonlawyers. Some of these employees provide services to the clients and bill the client for those services. Others provide services primarily to the lawyers and the rest of the law firm. No book could contain a list and description of every type of nonlawyer law firms employ. Here is a limited selection of some of the typical roles and responsibilities.

Billing Nonlawyers

Paralegals. A paralegal is a person who assists a lawyer in the practice of law, but is not himself or herself a lawyer. Paralegals vary greatly by knowledge, experience, and education. Although voluntary paralegal certification programs are growing and gaining recognition, there are no set criteria or credential that makes someone a paralegal. Some paralegals may have a two-year college degree or less. Others have substantially more education, even having completed law school.

There are also few limits on exactly what a paralegal can do. A paralegal cannot practice law, which in most jurisdictions means a paralegal cannot take or defend a deposition, appear as an advocate in court, hold himself or herself out as a lawyer, or give independent legal advice. However, paralegals are often permitted and do interview prospective clients, prepare legal documents or pleadings for an attorney to review, manage or prepare summaries of documents, investigate, and conduct research. The exact limits on paralegal practice vary widely depending upon how a jurisdiction defines the practice and unauthorized practice of law.

Some firms treat nurse paralegals as a separate category of paralegal. A nurse paralegal is normally a person with a nursing degree or other healthcare experience who serves as a paralegal. Often nurse paralegals provide specialized assistance on medical malpractice, health law, or similar matters.

A "law clerk," meanwhile, is often a person who is studying to become a lawyer, but has not yet passed the bar or obtained a law license in the relevant jurisdiction. Law clerks are often grouped more with the lawyers and billed to clients at higher rates; in actuality, however, they are often just another type of paralegal.

According to Altman Weil, law firms typically employ about one paralegal for every four lawyers. For larger firms, this number drops to about one paralegal for every five lawyers.[45] Also, as previously noted, some types of law firms—collection firms or certain types of plaintiff personal injury firms, for example—may employ one or more paralegal for each lawyer at the firm.

Research Specialists or Law Librarians. As law firm libraries have shrunk due to cost and growth of electronic resources, many law librarians have evolved into research specialists. They use their training (often a college or graduate degree focused on library and information management) to locate information for clients, and often bill for their time performing such research. Research specialists then provide this information to others, often to lawyers or paralegals, for use in particular matters.

---

[45] James D. Cotterman, *New Survey Provides Snapshot of Law Firm Economics Across U.S.* (Aug. 2, 2007).

Specialists. Specialists are a growing category of nonlawyers, particularly at large or specialized law firms. The title "specialist" normally refers to a law firm employee who has specialized knowledge, often an advanced degree, in a non-law related field, and who uses that knowledge to assist the attorneys. For example, a law firm may employ an economist to assist on antitrust matters, or a scientist or engineer to assist with patent or product liability matters. Often, these specialists bill clients directly, and provide services akin to those provided by paralegals. The services tend to be more specialized, and are often billed to clients at higher rates.

Non-Billing Employees

In addition to the billing employees, who work primarily or entirely on client matters, most law firms have several types of non-billing nonlawyer employees. These include:

Firm Administrator. This book uses the title "firm administrator" to refer to the person who oversees the administration and operation of the firm. "Administration and operation" refer to non-billable, non-client service operations of the firm, and ordinarily include budgeting, billing, collections, information technology, human resources (including hiring, training, managing and evaluating nonlawyer staff), facilities, and the like. At many firms, administration and operations may also include marketing and recruiting, although sometimes these functions are overseen by lawyers. At a more sophisticated firm, the firm administrator may also have a strategic role. The direct responsibilities of the firm administrator narrow as the firm employs other specialists to address other needs, until ultimately large firm administrators serve primarily as managers of managers.

Firm administrators generally report directly to a firm's capital partners, managing partner or management committee. Firms refer to their administrator by a number of titles, which include "chief operating officer," "executive director," "firm director," "legal administrator," and "managing director." Generally firm administrators are not lawyers, although sometimes a non-practicing lawyer may fill this role.

Firm administrators typically change as a firm moves through stages of growth and complexity. The initial firm administrator is often a very capable legal assistant/secretary or paralegal who assumes additional responsibilities. Later, a firm may retain someone with a business degree or management experience to manage a firm. Ultimately, larger or more sophisticated (or complex) firms may hire someone with significant management experience—often a former accounting firm partner or c-level executive (*e.g.*, chief executive officer or chief operating officer) from a company, or the like—to assume the top administrative position.

Authority delegated to firm administrators varies greatly. At some firms, the firm administrator is well respected and has great responsibility and authority. The firm administrator may even have some input on lawyer administration. At other firms, the firm administrator has little delegated authority. In fact, at some firms the lawyers may undercut the firm administrator, rendering the firm administrator largely ineffective.

Legal Secretaries or Assistants. At many firms, a lawyer receives assistance from a legal secretary or assistant with document preparation, scheduling, transcription, filing, and administration matters (including billing, client intake, and the like). Some firms also have secretaries manage client or firm files. The qualifications, abilities, and responsibility of such a secretary or assistant vary both within a firm and among firms. Many have a college degree or some college.

The exact authority and responsibilities of a secretary often vary depending upon the needs and practices of the lawyer or lawyers they assist. More senior lawyers often rely heavily on their secretaries or assistants to transcribe dictation, prepare documents, and manage the lawyer's schedule. More junior lawyers, however, are often quite adept at typing and using computers, and thus use secretaries primarily for finalizing documents or scheduling or administration matters.

Currently, law firms employ approximately one secretary for every two lawyers.[46] But a secretary's workload varies greatly de-

[46] James D. Cotterman, *New Survey Provides Snapshot of Law Firm Economics Across U.S.* (Aug. 2, 2007).

pending upon the lawyers (or at some firms paralegals) assisted. A secretary may serve only one senior lawyer, or a senior lawyer may have more than one secretary. Alternatively, a single secretary may assist a handful of more junior lawyers or paralegals, particularly when those junior lawyers are computer literate and prepare almost all of their documents by typing (not dictating).

The personal and professional relationships of secretaries can also be quite important. At some firm, the long-time secretary of a powerful senior partner may possess considerable authority in the firm because of this relationship. Additionally, a lawyer may build a very close relationship with a secretary or assistant. If such a relationship exists, a new lawyer who mistreats or shows disrespect for a treasured secretary or assistant may find his or her opportunities for success at the firm severely limited.

File Management. Lawyers require ready access to client information, research, and correspondence to do their jobs properly. The need for such ready access requires that client and matter files be carefully organized and managed, and many firms retain file management specialists to handle this file management.

Firms employ a number of different systems to accomplish this file organization and management. Some firms use a very centralized system, where all or most files are kept in a central filing area, often managed by file management personnel. Other firms may employ a decentralized system where each lawyer keeps his or her files separately. Often then files are managed by the lawyers' secretaries or legal assistants.

Some firms retain files in a paper format. Others are moving toward electronic file and document management systems. A sophisticated filing system may even include placing a bar code or radio frequency identification (RFID) tag on each portion of the file (red weld or file folder) so that it can be readily tracked, inventoried, and located.

Other Non-Billing Staff. Most other non-billing staff at law firms fill roles quite similar to what they would fill at non-law firms. This staff includes marketing, accounting, and information technology and are necessary for the smooth operation of a law firm. They are not described here in detail, however, because (except for marketing professionals, whose work is discussed later) their function largely approximates what they would do at any type of company.

12 Administrative Organizational Structures

Most law firm nonlawyer staff are arranged in one of two organizational structures. In the first structure, all nonlawyers who do not work directly with lawyers—that is, nonlawyers other than secretaries, paralegals, and specialists—usually report through the firm administrator to the managing partner or management committee. The basic structure for administrative functions often resembles the following:

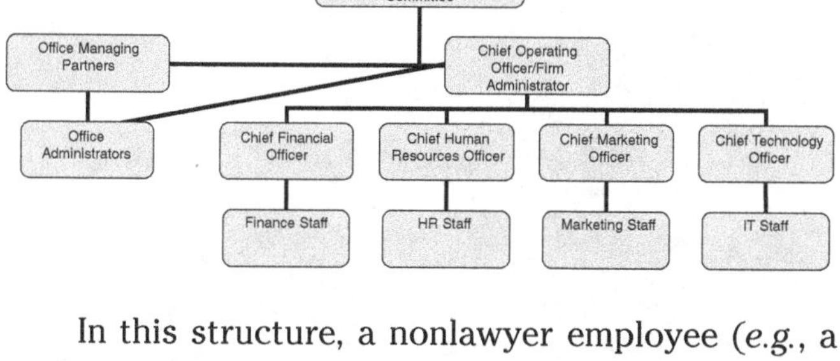

In this structure, a nonlawyer employee (*e.g.*, a marketing staff member) assigned to a secondary office may fall under the supervision of both the office administrator and the chief officer of that specialty. In other words, depending upon the firm and size of the office, an office administrator may manage the financial, marketing, technology, human resources, and other staff people who work in that office. Those employees may also report to the lead person in their department, who likely will reside in the firm's main office.

Note that this organizational chart does not include practicing lawyers. Practicing lawyers usually report through a wholly separate organizational structure. Examples of how lawyers are organized within a firm and on client matters are presented in Chapter 27.

More recently, firms have evolved so that those staff personnel who primarily serve the needs of the practicing lawyers—such as the marketing, strategy, and knowledge management staff—report through the practice structure instead of the administrative structure. Under this structure, the Chief Marketing Officer, for example, will not report to the Firm Administrator/Chief Operating Officer. Instead, the Chief Marketing Officer will report directly to the Managing Partner/Management Committee, so the lawyers may have a more direct working relationship with the marketing staff and vice versa.

13 Interactions with Nonlawyer Staff

A final note about the role of nonlawyers at law firms. Lawyers and firms sometimes show less regard for non-professionals than other employers. For example, lawyers—including this author in this text—typically describe the size of a firm by referring to the number of lawyers at the firm. We also tend to categorize everyone who works at a law firm but is not a lawyer as a "nonlawyer." Most professional organizations do not discuss their size only by referring to professionals, or refer to the non-professionals at the organization by using the prefix "non-." A hospital for example, does not relate its size by referring only to the number of doctors, or not refer to its employees as "doctors" and "non-doctors." Similarly, a bank does not describe its employees as "tellers" and "non-tellers." Such a lawyer-centric mindset may not be intended as a sign of disrespect; it may in fact be indicative of a problem, or at least seen as an indication of a problem. Also, it is not uncommon for law firms to treat lawyers or law clerks (i.e., law student interns) differently and much better than they treat everyone else. The lawyers may all go to lunch or pick up lunch for each other, for example, without ever considering inviting anyone else to participate. In fact, sometimes lawyers will hold events for summer law clerks and not invite others—who are students at the same law schools but serving in different roles (such as paralegals)—to participate.

To navigate a law firm safely and successfully, a junior lawyer probably should not let this attitude dominate his or her interactions with people at the firm. As discussed later, survival and success will often depend upon receiving assistance from the entire team, which will include both lawyers and nonlawyers. In addition, as suggested above in the discussion of legal secretaries or assistants, offending the wrong person—often the long-time and trusted paralegal or assistant of a powerful partner—may ensure that, despite a lawyer's best efforts, a lawyer will fail at a firm.

Further, lawyers should be mindful that they are responsible for the actions of the nonlawyers who assist them. Under Model Rule 5.3, any lawyer—even a junior lawyer—who is overseeing the work of a nonlawyer must make reasonable efforts to ensure the nonlawyer's conduct is compatible with the ethics rules. A lawyer who fails to do so may face professional discipline.

14 Partnership at XYZ Law Partnership, LLP—Exercise #1

The XYZ Law Partnership, LLP

The XYZ Law Partnership, LLP (XYZ) is a 60-lawyer firm based in Central City, with offices Downtown and in the Manufacturing District and in the Business District. (Each of these districts has its own courthouse, and is located about 20-30 minutes from Downtown.) XYZ primarily represents business entities in business transactions, real estate, and commercial litigation. It also has an employment law practice, an intellectual property group (with one equity partner patent attorney), and a tax practice. Total revenues are about $36 million.

XYZ's real estate group has an excellent reputation and represents several major developers. The firm has also historically rated very high for its employment and tax practices, but recently its employment practice has been hurt by the increase in insurance coverage for employment matters and the (somewhat related) decline in billing rates. The firm's IP practice developed into a practice group in 2001-02. Although the attorneys are all capable, the intellectual property practice has not taken off. Hours for people practicing in the department normally hover at about 1,500 to 1,600 per year. Several IP associates have moved to other departments due to the lack of work and opportunities for significant experience. With the exception of Quinton Quarles' bankruptcy litigation practice, the litigation practice largely feeds off the real estate, business transactions, and tax practices.

XYZ has a two-tier partnership. Associates are normally considered for non-equity partnership after seven years. Except for exceptional candidates, lawyers spend about three to five years as a non-equity partner before being considered for elevation to equity partnership. The firm's partnership agreement and operating policies also allow a lawyer to move directly from associate to equity partner, but this has never happened.

XYZ has five lawyers that are "Counsel" to the firm. One is Mark Mudd, former managing partner of the Mudd Law Group (MLG), who is semi-retired (but still bills about 2,100 hours a year). His regular billing rate of $550 per hour is the highest in the firm.[47] The other four counsel are lawyers who were passed over for partnership the last few years, except for Alice Adams in Business District, who works part-time and was deemed not eligible for partnership on this basis.

The Business District office largely consists of the former MLG. MLG merged into XYZ in 2003. The Business District office is the most expensive, but also has higher billing rates. The only non-MLG lawyers in the office are two brand new associates (in tax and business transactions), and a third-year associate in the real estate practice. Also, recently a former MLG equity litigation partner, Julie January, left the Business District office to set up her own firm. January was a major rainmaker and the office managing partner. She took a non-equity partner and two associates, all from the Business District office, with her when she left.

Until recently, the Manufacturing District office had a significant asbestos defense practice. The firm released one non-equity

[47]Rates in this scenario are based on national averages. In some locations, billing rates for lawyers would vary greatly from the rates used in this example. *See infra* Chapter 19.

partner and two associates from that office after the firm lost its major asbestos client, Acme Manufacturing Company, in 2007 due to a business conflict.

The firm has Compensation, Management, Recruiting, Risk Management, Technology Committee, Diversity, and Associate Development Committees.

Highest Business Origination in 2008

Lawyer	Position	Practice	Office	Originations
Mark Mudd	Of Counsel	Real Estate	Business District	$6,200,000
Noah Newton	Equity Partner	Tax	Downtown/ Business District	$2,600,000
Oliver Opperman	Equity Partner	Real Estate	Downtown	$2,100,000
Paula Peterson	Equity Partner	Business Services	Downtown	$1,800,000
Quinton Quarles	Equity Partner	Litigation	Downtown	$1,700,000
Rene Rollins	Equity Partner	Real Estate	Business District	$1,700,000
			Total	**$16,100,000**

Firm Leaders (all equity partners)

Hal Hinton	Member of Management Committee Head of Employment Practice
Noah Newton	Member of Management Committee Head of Tax Practice Member of Compensation Committee
Oliver Opperman	Managing Partner Head of Downtown Office Member of Compensation Committee
Paula Peterson	Member of Management Committee Head of Business Transactions Practice Head of Diversity Committee Member of Compensation Committee
Quinton Quarles	Member of Management Committee Head of Litigation Practice Member of Compensation Committee
Rene Rollins	Member of Management Committee Head of Real Estate Practice Head of Business District Office Member of Compensation Committee
Stan Sanders	Head of Manufacturing District Office Lawyer in Business Transactions Practice

There are also two more junior equity partners on the Compensation Committee.

The practices, median rate paid (MRP) per hour, and median hours realized (MHR)[48] for the firm's lawyers are as follows:

Practice	Partners (Equity)	Counsel	Associates	Total
Real Estate	8 (6)* MRP: $340 MHR: 1800	2 MRP: $425 MHR: 1900	4 MRP: $220 MHR: 1950	14
Litigation	7 (6) MRP: $320 MHR: 1900	2* MRP: $310 MHR: 1700	4 MRP: $200 MHR: 1800	13
Business Transactions	8 (7) MRP: $340 MHR: 1800	0	10 MRP: $240 MHR: 1870	18
Employment	3 (3) MRP: $270 MHR: 1800	0 MHR: 2200	3 MRP: $210	6
Intellectual Property	2 (1) MRP: $420 MHR: 1580	1 MRP: $350 MHR: 1600	2 MRP: $320 MHR: 1500	5
Tax	2 (1) MRP: $440 MHR: 2150	0 MHR: 2100	2 MRP: $290	4
Total:	30 (24)	5	25	60

*One non-equity real estate partner and one litigation counsel are not full time. Their hours and rate paid are projected to reflect full-time equivalents.

[48]This chart uses "median rate paid" and "median hours realized" so the numbers are the "real" numbers: what people actually received after write downs, write offs, and other billing issues were resolved. For example, if a lawyer bills 2000 hours at $300 per hour, but clients only pays for 1,800 hours at $300 per hour, this chart reflects only the 1,800 hours realized. All other references to billable hours in this exercise are hours realized.

Diversity: Diverse lawyers at the firm are as follows:

	Total	Caucasian	African American	Asian American	Hispanic
Equity Partners	24	21	1	1	1
Male	17	15	1		1
Female	7	6		1	
Non-Equity Partners	6	5	1		
Male	3	3			
Female	3	2	1		
Of Counsel	5	4		1	
Male	2	2			
Female	3	2		1	
Associates	25	20	3	1	1
Male	11	8	1	1	1
Female	14	12	2		

Traditionally, XYZ has struggled to keep diverse attorneys more than MLG did. MLG had an excellent history of keeping and promoting female attorneys, including that Julie January had risen to head MLG's litigation practice before the merger (Mudd himself was head of MLG's transactional practice). Particularly in light of January's departure, several former MLG lawyers including Mark Mudd, Noah Newton, and Rene Rollins have voiced concern with the firm's efforts to encourage female and diverse attorneys to stay with the firm. To answer such concerns, Paula Peterson (head of Business Transactions) was recently asked to chair the diversity committee.

Location of Offices: All lawyers are in the Downtown office except:

Business District Office

Practice	Partners (Equity)	Counsel	Associates	Total
Real Estate	6 (4)*	1	3	9
Litigation	0	2*	2	4
Business	2 (2)	0	2	4
Tax	.5 (.5)	0	1	1.5
Total:	8.5 (6.5)	3	8	18.5

The part-time litigation counsel Alice Adams works in the Business District office. Also, tax partner Noah Newton splits his time between the Downtown and Business District offices.

Manufacturing District Office

Practice	Partners (Equity)	Counsel	Associates	Total
Litigation	1 (1)	0	1	2
Business	1 (1)	0	1	2
Total:	2 (2)	0	2	4

Part A—Who should be made equity partner?

The firm needs to evaluate who should be made equity partner in 2010. Due to lack of increased revenue in 2009, the partnership has indicated no more than two candidates should be equitized. The firm administrator, however, believes the firm may accept three candidates if a compelling case is made. The Compensation Committee is considering four candidates for recommendation to the partnership: Alice Adams, Bruce Benning, Caroline Clifford, and David Donovan.

Alice Adams is a counsel and real estate litigator in the Business District office. She has not previously been considered for partnership because she works only 70 percent time. She was nominated by Rene Rollins, head of the Business District office, at the request of Mark Mudd.

A Central City native, Adams graduated from Central City University and in 1995 from Notre Dame Law School. She then joined MLG, where she represented developers in real-estate related litigation. She went part-time in 2004 after the birth of her second child, shortly before MLG merged into XYZ. She worked under Julie January, and January asked Adams to join her when January left XYZ to start her own firm. Adams decided to remain with XYZ, however, after Mark Mudd promised that Adams would be considered for partnership in January 2010.

Adams currently works 70 percent of full-time. She billed 1,500 hours average each of the last three years. Her hours realized and average rate paid for 2008 were 1,400 and $360 per hour respectively ($504,000 gross revenues). She originated $330,000 in business in 2009, down from about $400,000 in 2008. Previously, Adams had consistently originated at least $300,000 in business each of the past four years.

In 2009, Adams received very good reviews from her supervisors (including Julie January) and subordinates. Also, recent client interviews revealed that clients believe she has very good legal skills and professional judgment. But she never served in a leadership position, having always worked under January. Mudd has indicated that he believes the firm needs an equity partner to handle the real estate litigation, or XYZ will jeopardize its relationship with major real estate developers. Mudd also saw to it that Adams was appointed to serve on the Diversity Committee with Paula Peterson. Peterson has been impressed with Adams' work on the Diversity Committee and has said the promotion of Alice Adams is important to demonstrate that the firm will take care of part-time attorneys.

Adams is active with the Notre Dame Law School alumni, and she speaks 2-3 times per year at national meetings for real estate developers on litigation developments. Adams has lukewarm support from the Litigation Department: most of them say they have never worked on any matter with her because January's practice was so insular. The Litigation Department had another candidate they wanted to push through in 2010 but this candidate did not make the initial cut.

Adams is married to an architect. They have two children. Adams is Caucasian.

Bruce Benning is a Business Transactions associate in the downtown office. He should be up for non-equity partner this year, but Paula Peterson (head of the Business Transactions Practice) requested that Benning be considered for equity partner as well because Peterson knows Benning has been attracting interest from larger firms. Benning graduated from Yale University and Cornell Law School in 2002. He joined XYZ immediately after law school, and has been active on the firm's Technology Committee since 2006.

A Central City native, Benning has established himself as the firm's expert on start-up funding for technology companies. In

2008, he was also recognized as an *Influential Technology Leader* for his work in obtaining funding for Digital Images, a Central City electronic records management company that is among the region's fastest companies.

Benning billed 1,800 hours realized in 2009, with an average rate paid of $300 ($540,000 gross revenues). Peterson has also asked the firm to remember that he billed almost 200 hours to a firm client that declared bankruptcy, and that the firm wrote off these hours. Benning originated about $400,000 in 2009. This was his strongest year for business development; previously, he had not developed more than $250,000 in business.

Benning is well-liked by his supervisors, but is perceived as overly driven by some peers and subordinates. Clients generally like him and feel he does good work, but some smaller clients complain they feel neglected by him. Finally, the firm's risk management partner has complained that sometimes Benning agrees to work and begins working for clients before conflict checks and client engagement requirements are completed.

Benning is not married. He has had a several year on-again, off-again relationship with a woman he met at Cornell, who is now a government lawyer in Washington, DC. Benning is Caucasian.

Caroline Clifford is a non-equity partner in the Tax Practice Downtown. She graduated from Neighboring State University and, in 1997, its law school. She completed an LL.M. in Tax at New York University in 2000. She has published several articles and frequently speaks locally and nationally on partnership tax issues. She has also taught a class on tax law to business school students at Central City College, and was recently appointed to a Regional Commerce and Growth Association panel studying how tax laws could be changed to cultivate economic growth in Central City.

A Neighboring State native, Clifford joined XYZ in 1997 as a Business Transactions associate. After completing her LL.M., she moved to the Tax group.

Clifford had 2,200 hours realized at an average rate of $400 in 2009 ($800,000 gross revenues): everything she billed was collected in full. She has originated at least $400,000 in business each of the last three years (since she was made non-equity partner), and originated about $460,000 in 2009. She has no single major client, but receives referrals from a large number of accountants and financial advisors to handle complex tax matters.

Clifford is pleasant but very quiet and introverted; in fact, some lawyers express surprise that she still works at the firm because she is something of a stealth lawyer. Noah Newton has made clear that he believes Clifford should be an equity partner.

Clifford divorced in 2006 and is not currently dating anyone seriously. She has no children. Clifford is African American.

David Donovan is a second-year non-equity partner in the Intellectual Property group. He graduated from prestigious Central City Preparatory Academy, Massachusetts Institute of Technology, and, in 1998, University of Chicago Law School. He practiced briefly in Chicago, and then moved to Central City in 2001. He joined XYZ in 2001 as a litigation associate, and then became its copyright and trademark specialist starting in 2003.

Donovan is from an established Central City legal family; his father was acting general counsel of Central City Bank briefly in the 1980s, and recently retired from Central City's largest law firm. His sister is a partner at another major Central City law firm. Donovan had 1,500 hours realized in 2009 at an average rate of $380 ($570,000 gross revenues). He originated $600,000 in 2009, and has originated at least $350,000 each year for the past three years. At least half this work is for other practice groups.

Although he tends to avoid firm social events, Donovan is well liked by superiors, peers, subordinates and clients. But clients sometimes express concern that he bills too much time on particular matters, and about 10 percent of his time is written off each year on this basis. He is a good mentor and team player. He was an associate representative on the firm's Associate Development Committee, and currently serves on the firm's Recruiting Committee.

Donovan has strong support from his department (*i.e.*, the other IP partner), who has voiced concerns that Donovan needs to make equity partner to help the IP group continue to grow. The other IP partner has also expressed concern that Donovan may leave if he does not make equity partner this year.

Donovan is married to a former teacher and had his first child in 2008. Having a child has not had a noticeable impact on his work or work habits. Donovan is Caucasian.

Part B—Should any of the following equity partners be de-equitized?

The partnership at XYZ has also asked the Compensation Committee to determine whether one or more partners should be evaluated for de-equitization (demotion to non-equity partner) in 2009. Again, there are four candidates: Eileen Elton, Francisco Fernandez, Greg Gilmore, and Hal Hinton.

Eileen Elton, Litigation Department, Downtown Office. Elton joined the firm immediately after law school and was made an equity partner in 2001 based upon her solid billable hours and dutiful service to Quinton Quarles. She bills 2,100 or more hours every year, and averaged more than $300 per hour paid in 2008. (Her gross revenues for 2008 were $680,000.) However, she has never originated more than $300,000 in business.

Elton is a very hard worker. Everyone at the firm respects her, and she gets along well with clients. Elton has also served on the firm's Risk Management Committee since 2004. She is 47 years old, married, and has four children, including two in college.

Elton does not know that the firm is considering her for de-equitization. Quinton Quarles knows that the firm is considering de-equitizing Elton. He previously supported Elton's elevation, but now says the firm should make its own decision, and that he has other attorneys who could handle much of her work. However, Quarles is concerned that Elton might take one of his major clients (with revenue of about $250,000 per year) with her if she were to leave the firm. Elton is Caucasian.

Francisco Fernandez, Litigation, Manufacturing District office. Fernandez joined the firm in 1993 and managed the Manufacturing District office from 2000 to 2008. In 2008, he lost his major client Acme Manufacturing Company after the firm—against Fernandez's recommendation—agreed to represent Acme's competitor Heavy Industries in a major business acquisition where Acme had also sought to acquire the target company. For more than a decade, Acme had provided more than $1 million per year in revenue related to asbestos defense.

Fernandez billed and collected 1,850 hours at $320 per hour ($592,000 in gross revenue) in 2009. He originated about $550,000 in business, better than would have been expected after his loss of Acme.

Before the loss of Acme, Fernandez was well liked and well respected, and he ran the Manufacturing District office very efficiently. After the loss of Acme, Fernandez has alternated between being helpful and causing trouble, mainly by questioning and undermining firm management. Fernandez has fought very hard to maintain his pre-Acme compensation. Mudd never liked Fernandez and asked that Fernandez be put on the de-equitization list.

Fernandez is 50 years old, married, and has two children—one in college, one out of college. Fernandez is Hispanic.

If Fernandez leaves, he will likely take all or virtually all of his clients with him. He would also likely take a very good and loyal paralegal with him.

Greg Gilmore, Business Services, Downtown Office. Gilmore is a well-respected banking attorney who graduated from Harvard Law School, joined the firm as a non-equity partner in 2004, and made equity partner in 2006. He has originated about $1,200,000 in business each year since 2004. In 2008, he had 1,900 hours realized at an average rate of $360, for $684,000 in gross revenue. Such a performance is consistent with his work since 2004.

Gilmore does a considerable amount of public speaking, including for national organizations. He was an *Influential Business Leader* recognized by the *Central City Journal* in 2004, the year he joined the firm, and he helped Benning earn an award in 2008. Gilmore was also named to the *Business Journal's Young Business Leader* list in 2002.

While Gilmore treats clients and fellow partners well, he is generally sarcastic and demeaning to those he deems as beneath him. When under pressure, Gilmore has a quick, nasty temper that usually includes hurling a barrage of obscenities (and sometimes office supplies) at subordinates who fail to satisfy his ridiculous and unspoken expectations. He has gone through eight secretaries since 2004, including having two walk out on him during major loan closings. Five associates have cited Gilmore's behavior as the reason they left XYZ. The firm had Gilmore work with a personality coach in 2008–09, but it has not helped. Gilmore has been warned that the firm will consider demoting him or firing him.

If he leaves, Gilmore will take all his business with him—which would leave two associates and a paralegal with very little to do. Gilmore is 45 years old. He is divorced twice and may remarry soon. He has three children, all by his first wife. Gilmore is Caucasian.

Hal Hinton, Employment, Downtown office. Hinton serves on the management committee and heads the employment practice. He has practiced employment law for more than 29 years, including 17 at XYZ, and is 57 years old.

As of 2006, Hinton consistently originated more than $1.5 million per year, almost all providing labor and employment counsel for the General Motors plant in Suburbia. But GM put the work out for bid, and Hinton was undercut by a national employment law firm that recently opened a Suburbia office. In 2009, he originated $300,000 in business. His hours realized and average fees paid were 1650 and $300 respectively, for $478,500 in gross revenues. His hours, revenue, and business originated were the lowest of any Employment Group partner.

Hinton has always spoken and written extensively in the employment law field. Since losing GM, he has remained upbeat and has been trying to reposition himself as an employee benefits attorney since 2006. This has not yet yielded much business, but Hinton often voices promise that it will.

Hinton is very well liked by the XYZ partnership and staff, except the Business District office (Mudd and his former MLG colleagues) complains that Hinton is overcompensated and has not been pulling his weight. Hinton is very good at working with and developing younger lawyers.

During his compensation meetings since 2005, Hinton has expressed concern that employment law rates have declined and that traditional labor work has all but disappeared. He has also said that he is consistently losing work to lawyers who charge lower rates for employment law work, or handle employment cases for insurance companies whose reimbursement rates are too low for XYZ.

Hinton knows that the firm is considering de-equitizing partners, but he has not been told that he is on the list. If Hinton were to leave, he could take as much as the entire employment law practice with him.

Hinton is married. He has no children. Hinton is Caucasian.

Criteria for Partnership at XYZ

There are no formal criteria for promotion to equity partnership. However, the Compensation Committee, which has responsibility to equitize and de-equitize any partner as well as to set compensation for all equity and non-equity partners, has established "threshold considerations," which are:

- Respect from the firm
- Respect from the legal community at large
- Origination of business
- Commitment to clients
- Commitment to the firm

Although there is no formal threshold, ordinarily an equity partner is expected to originate more than $400,000 per year in legal work.

Comment on Exercise #1

Details regarding race, age, marital status, and education are included to provide additional factors for consideration. They may be altered or removed as appropriate.

Additional information for this Exercise, including an instructor supplement, is available at **www.DowneyonLawPractice.com**.

The Market for Legal Services

15

The approximately $200 billion market for legal services[49] in the United States is not too dissimilar from the market for other professional services. A large amount of need exists for lawyers who can provide relatively basic services to consumers at low cost. Such services include, for example, handling residential real estate closings in states where a lawyer's assistance is required; helping people prepare basic wills and trusts; handling basic lawsuits; and forming corporations.[50] The amount of need declines as the

---

[49]*See* U.S. Census Bureau, *Legal Services 2002*, available at **http://www.census.gov/prod/ec02/ec0254i01.pdf** (estimating the legal services industry in 2002 at $182 billion in gross receipts).

[50]Many complain that lawyers do not do a good job of meeting the broad need for low-cost consumer legal services. A 2005 study by the Legal Services Corporation estimated that approximately 80 percent of low-income Americans who need legal assistance on civil matters do not receive it. Evelyn Nieves, *80% of Poor Lack Civil Legal Aid, Study Says*, Washington Post, at A09 (Oct. 15, 2005) (reporting on "Documenting the Justice Gap in America"); *see also* Illinois Legal Aid, *Severely Under-funded Legal Aid Agencies Operating Under Emergency "Triage" System* (Feb. 8, 2005) (reporting a

legal services become more complex, but prospective clients seeking these more complex services will often pay more for those services. Finally, a few clients seek elite, specialized services and will pay (virtually) any price for those services. The lawyer retained to prepare Bill Gates' will, for example, would likely face a very complex challenge. Gates would also likely anticipate paying more than the $500 to $2000 or so that many lawyers charge for basic estate-planning documents.

Hildebrandt International, a major consultant to law firms, has developed a diagram to represent the market for legal services—from the client's perspective. That graphic is:

Exhibit—Market for Legal Services[51]

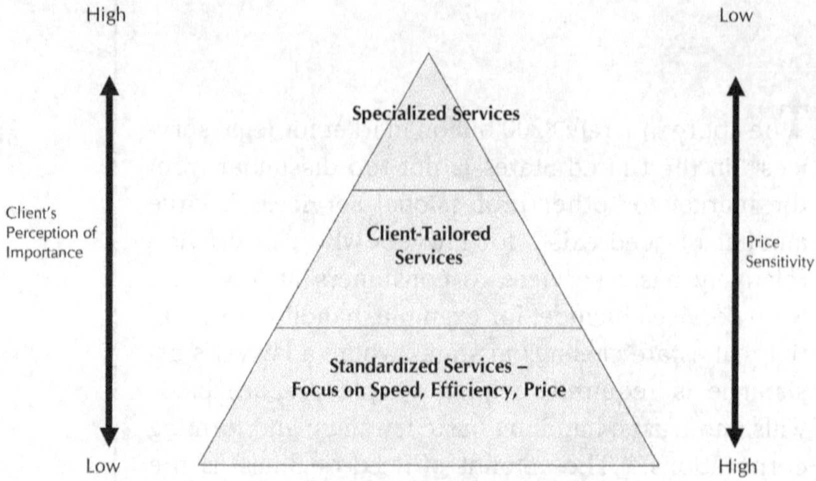

statewide survey in Illinois found a similar shortage in legal aid). This shortfall may be alleviated to some degree by the development in the late 2000s of law school and federal programs to help newer lawyers who enter legal services and similar practices to repay their law school loans. The long-term effects of such programs, however, remain uncertain at the time this text is being published.

[51]This model is modified from the model published in *Hildebrandt Handbook of Law Firm Management* 6-5 (2005) and through other Hildebrandt materials such as William Johnson's June 2006 presentation *Drivers of Financial Performance and Peculiarities of Law Firm Economics.*

This model focuses on the value a client places on a legal matter. Such determinations must be made on a case-by-case basis, because a particular client might value a particular matter very differently than how that client would view other matters, or how other clients might view the same matter. For example, a typical client may view the handling of a minor legal dispute as not significant. A politician seeking to avoid scandal, however, may consider that same legal dispute a major potential headache, and be willing to expend more resources to resolve the dispute quickly and quietly.

Also, a small closely held business may view an employment discrimination lawsuit, particularly its first such suit, as a major problem requiring the best counsel. A major global company that has been sued for employment discrimination hundreds or thousands of times, however, may see a discrimination claim by a former low-level employee as a minor problem, one that should be resolved efficiently and effectively. Of course, that same global company might view a discrimination case by a former executive that is generating harmful publicity or a class action suit as a more significant matter, one where the company would pay a premium to receive more specialized legal representation.

A particular type of law practice typically moves down the value pyramid—or becomes "commoditized"—over time. When a new legal problem first presents itself, clients are more likely to see that type of matter as significant because the risks are largely unknown. Also, fewer lawyers and nonlawyers are prepared to handle such matters. The lawyer who develops expertise in addressing that matter is perceived as having a relatively rare and often valuable specialty. Over time, however, lawyers and clients generally become more accustomed to dealing with the legal issues, and the perceived value and associated rates for those types of legal issues typically decline. Such commoditization can have major consequences both for law firms and individual lawyers.

An example of a practice undergoing such commoditization is defending employment discrimination litigation. In the 1980s and early 1990s, employment litigation cases were increasing and were perceived as higher value work. Corporate-focused law firms often developed strong practices and saw such practices as an important aspect of their service to corporate clients. In the past decade or so, however, many clients have become quite accustomed to employment discrimination claims. Corporations purchase insurance that often covers the defense and resolution of such claims, or they handle many aspects of such claims in-house. Also, nonlaw firm providers such as investigation and consulting firms now provide many employment-law related services other than those directly related to litigation, generally at lower rates than law firms typically charge. These factors have generally caused a decline in supply and typical billing rates for defending many types of employment discrimination claims. In the early 2000s, meanwhile, some larger corporate-focused firms were pressuring senior lawyers to increase billing rates. These conflicting pressures caused many employment discrimination defense litigators to move to smaller or specialty firms. Other employment discrimination litigators responded to such pressures by altering their practices, for example evolving into a focus on counseling to avoid claims or handling employee benefits litigation claims, a newer sub-specialty where, at least at the time, rates remained higher.

A similar commoditization has occurred with environmental compliance work. Initially, lawyers had an effective monopoly on the provision of environmental compliance services: they could read and interpret the statutes and help companies and others address environmental compliance issues, generally for the first time. Over time, however, regulators, regulated entities, and their (often non-lawyer) professionals became more accustomed to dealing with ensuring compliance, filing reports, and the like. Now, in-house environmental compliance departments or environmental engineering firms frequently provide many of the services that lawyers once provided but at lower rates. Some attorneys still practicing in the area have moved to higher-rate, more specialized niches of the practice, such as dealing with the special problems that may arise, or advising companies about how to deal with new environmental law issues. But others have lost revenue or modified their practices to avoid direct competition with lower cost, nonlawyer providers.

It is important not to read more from this diagram than it is intended to represent. First, this diagram does not define fixed strata for law firms or law practices. Most lawyers and firms have practices that are located in multiple areas and at multiple levels of the value triangle. For example, a general practice lawyer—particularly one in an area served by few lawyers—may handle a wide variety of matters that are scattered all over the value pyramid. Such a lawyer may defend minor criminal charges, file personal bankruptcies, and prepare simple wills, generally activities at the lower portions of the value pyramid. But the same general practitioner may also prepare more complex wills, prosecute complicated medical malpractice cases, and defend against serious felony charges, activities generally placed higher on the value pyramid. Even lawyers or firms who focus their practice on a particular type of case often have matters located in different portions of the value pyramid. A lawyer or firm that litigates personal injury or commercial cases will often have some high value cases and some low-value cases. A law firm that prepares wills, defends criminal prosecutions, or handles corporate transactions would also generally have a mix of higher- and lower-value work.

In light of these considerations, a commercial litigation or business transaction practice at a particular firm may be suitable to diagram as follows:

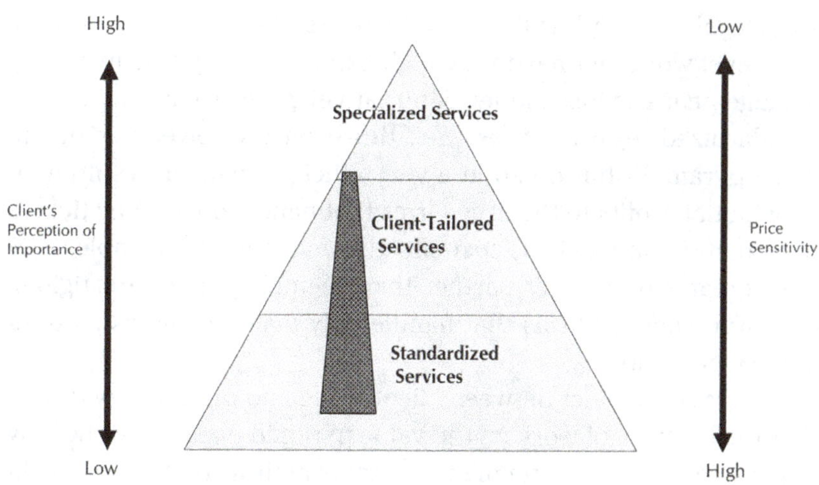

The shaded quadrangle represents the practice, which includes more lower-value, standardized work and less higher-value, more specialized work. Often such a mix of work may be a practical necessity. A lawyer or firm may conclude that it can only focus its practice on a particular type of case by handling both run-of-the-mill and specialized legal services for that type of matter. Also, clients often seek specialized services from the same law firm that is already providing less specialized services. For example, a company may select a law firm already representing it on relatively minor employment matters to handle a more complex, specialized employment matter. A firm that does not provide more standardized services may find itself effectively foreclosed from consideration when such a client requires more specialized services.

Of course, some firms will try to focus only on a tier or portion of the value triangle. For example, a firm that handles collections, traffic violations, or residential real estate closings may focus primarily on the lower portion of the triangle. A firm that focuses in high-profile divorces, white collar criminal defense, or very complex tax and estate planning matters, meanwhile, may restrict its work only to matters that it perceives as being near the top of the value pyramid. In reality, such focused practices remain relatively rare.

The second limitation of the value pyramid is that it displays only clients' perceived value of legal work, not the profitability of such legal work. A law firm may focus its practice solely on very high level work, but have very high expenses or engage in sloppy management and lose money. Alternatively, a firm may handle only standardized legal services (*i.e.*, those on the lower tier of the value pyramid), but do so in a very efficient manner, resulting in substantial profits to the firm. Firms that handle only traffic tickets but do so in an efficient, cost-effective manner, for example, may have greater profits per partner than seemingly more prestigious corporate-focused firms that handle only major, complex matters at very high rates.

This disconnect between client value and profitability means that the location of work on the value pyramid does not show how much lawyers at that firm make. Partners at firms that handle high-volume, primarily low-value worker's compensation and minor personal injury cases may make more than partners at the largest corporate-focused law firms in the same city. As discussed in Chapter 19, these higher profits are often the result of higher leverage and lower overhead expenses.

Client Control and Convergence

Consumers of legal services vary as much as providers in the $200 billion market for legal services. Some consumers have virtually no experience with lawyers, and may retain a lawyer only once in their lives. Other clients, particularly large corporations and insurers, may have hundreds or thousands of lawyers both inside and outside the company performing their legal work every day. In-house legal departments can and sometimes will carefully track everything that happens in a representation and dictate numerous aspects of the attorney-client relationship. This may include which lawyers at which firms provide services, as well as many of the terms under which such services are provided.

Clients often have the ability to exert considerable influence over their legal counsel. Some of this client influence reflects that lawyers act as agents and owe fiduciary responsibilities to their clients. The influence a client should have over its lawyer is also reflected in the ABA Model Rules of Professional Conduct, in particular Model Rule 1.2.

Yet recent trends support that some client influence also comes from the market power major recipients of legal services can yield. Three recent movements by in-house counsel in particular demonstrate that some institutional clients recognize and are attempting to exert their market power.

First, in the 1990s, several legal departments, including those at Marriott International, Inc. and E.I. du Pont de Nemours and Co., decided to significantly reduce the number of law firms they used. This practice is referred to as "convergence." The impact of convergence can be quite substantial. Marriott, for example, used over 200 law firms in December 1994, but quickly reduced that number to 10.[52] "[C]onvergers expect[ed] a number of benefits

[52]Tamara Loomis, *Closed Club*, Corporate Counsel (Aug. 19, 2005), *available at* **http://www.law.com/jsp/ihc/PubArticleFriendlyIHC.jsp?id=1124269516213**.

from a smaller panel of key firms. Those firms, they believe, [would] know the company better, impose less of a management burden in keeping track of transaction costs, offer better billing terms, and contribute special services."[53]

Not everyone agrees that such convergence provides the desired benefits.[54] But companies that have converged typically continue to use the limited number of firms that made the cut.[55] And further, companies continue to reduce the number of outside legal providers they use. In 2007, Tyco International announced it was reducing its outside legal counsel for Europe, Africa, and the Middle East from 250 firms to 1, Eversheds LLP.[56]

Second, in the 2000s, a number of legal departments including Shell Oil Company and Sara Lee Corporation began to push outside counsel to improve the number and role of diverse lawyers in their firms and particularly within their partnerships. This movement has spread to other corporate legal departments, including McKesson Corporation and Walmart.[57] Clients advocating greater diversity began to ask about diversity statistics when selecting counsel or deciding which counsel to retain. Some clients also set standards for the participation of diverse lawyers on their matters, in particular seeking confirmation that diverse lawyers were given opportunity to participate in a significant fashion on such matters. A few clients even offered bonuses to firms that increased the diversity of their firm leadership, or the diversity of the lawyers who provided service to those clients. The results of such efforts remain uncertain, although a number of firms

---

[53]Rees W. Morrison, *Don't Put All Your Eggs in One Basket*, Legal Times (Apr. 10, 2006), available at **http://www.hildebrandt.com/Documents.aspx?Doc_ID=2432**.

[54]For a critique of convergence, *see id.*

[55]Tamara Loomis, *Closed Club*, Corporate Counsel (Aug. 19, 2005).

[56]*See Press Release: Tyco International and Eversheds LLP announce innovative corporate legal and governance initiative* (Jan. 10, 2007), *available at* **http://www.eversheds.com/uk/Home/Articles/index.page?ArticleID=templatedata\Eversheds\articles\data\en\Tyco_International_and_Eversheds_LLP_announce_innovative_corporate_legal_and_governance_initiative**.

[57]Kellie Schmitt, *Corporate Diversity Demands Put Pressure on Outside Counsel*, The Recorder (Dec. 28, 2006), *available at* **http://www.law.com/jsp/ihc/PubArticleIHC.jsp?id=1167214010196**.

were reported to have responded to pressures to diversify their partnerships by making rapid gains in promoting or hiring diverse lawyers.[58]

Third, a number of clients are now pressuring their law firms to replace time-based billing with alternative billing arrangements. Such efforts, as well as the results of such efforts, are discussed in greater detail in Chapter 17.

Strategic Alignment

Another trend that has impacted law firms and law firm management is a focus on strategic alignment of firm resources. Some law firms have made a concerted effort to pursue strategic alignment. These firms believe they will operate more efficiently and thus more profitably if they (a) identify what portion of the legal market they want to serve and (b) strategically align their resources to serve that market segment. Such firms ordinarily decide to focus on a particular segment of the market or type of legal matter. These firms then seek to align all their resources—including office locations, staff, research resources, client services, and the like—to promote that focus as efficiently and effectively as possible.

An apparent example of a consumer-focused firm that has attempted strategic alignment is Richard A. Ciummo & Associates ("RCA"), an 85-lawyer Fresno, California-based law firm that was featured in the 2007 article, *Calif. Defense Firm Borrows Wal-Mart Business Model* published in the legal newspaper *The Recorder.*[59] According to the article, RCA focuses on providing a "range of professional services at affordable prices" to local governments. These services included contracts totaling more than $40 million to provide criminal defense services to indigent defendants. The article states that RCA seeks to provide such services by "generating volume and cutting costs in ways [its] government-based counterparts can't and many private-sector competitors won't."

---

[58]*Id.*

[59]Cheryl Miller, *Calif. Defense Firm Borrows Wal-Mart Business Model,* The Recorder (Dec. 26, 2007).

For example, RCA generally does not raise salaries with experience, but it does allow lawyers to handle their own cases on the side. RCA also recruits primarily through the website Craigslist, not through law schools or summer associate programs.

The *Recorder* article also discusses how RCA obtains new clients:

> Ciummo said his business plan, which has focused largely on rural, Central Valley and foothill counties, doesn't rely on expansion. But county leaders continue to call him. Two administrators in counties with Ciummo contracts say they, too, have been contacted by other county officials asking about the firm's work.
>
> A pitch on his Web site says it all: "What would your county do with hundreds of thousands of dollars?"[60]

Apparently the only equity owner, Ciummo himself explains: "This is a high-volume, low-profit business for me. . . . It's more like a grocery store."[61]

A sharp contrast is the strategic focus of Wachtell Lipton Rosen & Katz, a leading Wall Street firm. Wachtell differs from other large Wall Street firms with regard to its size, its practice focus, its billing system, and its profitability. Wachtell is smaller than most other leading New York firms: it is generally the smallest of the *AmLaw 100* (or most profitable large corporate firms). Further, it has fewer associates per partner (or "lower leverage") than most other major corporate firms: while most corporate firms have two to four associates per lawyer, Wachtell has less than one associate per partner. Wachtell also tries to restrict its practice so that it avoids routine or labor-intensive legal work and instead serves corporations as special counsel on important, unusual litigation and transactional matters. This has become a benefit: Wachtell is perceived as a rare firm where corporations turn "when they are most desperate, when their normal legal resources seem inadequate; at least, when they do not want to find out

---

[60] *Id.*

[61] *Id.*

whether their normal legal resources would be adequate, or when they do not want to risk Wachtell's aiding their opponents."[62]

For such work, Wachtell generally does not bill by the hour. Instead, Wachtell apparently charges fees based upon the size of the transaction or the value clients receive from Wachtell's legal work.[63] Employing such billing methods, Wachtell generally ranks among the leading corporate firms for revenues per lawyer and profits per equity partner.[64]

Sometimes a particular practice will almost necessitate that it have a certain type of law firm platform. In July 2008, the *Legal Intelligencer* discussed whether *qui tam* practices—practices where whistleblowers seek to share in the recovery of misappropriated or misspent federal funds—work better at smaller firms. The article began:

> Large law firms have increasingly dabbled in the contingent-fee arena, representing corporate plaintiffs in large-scale matters, but there is one highly lucrative practice the firms can't seem to make work.[65]

The article suggested several possible reasons why large firms may have trouble incorporating a *qui tam* action. These include conflicts of interest, because suits are often brought against large government or corporate entities from whom corporate-focused firms often seek other work; and the required commitment of time and money, often without immediate compensation, that are required before the firm may have an opportunity to be compensated by sharing in the client's return, *i.e.*, the "feast or famine" nature of the work. Frank D'Amore of Attorney Career Catalysts

---

[62]William H. Starbuck, *Keeping a Butterfly and an Elephant in a House of Cards: The Elements of Exceptional Success*, 30 J. Management Studies 885 (1993).

[63]*Id.* Hourly and value billing are discussed in Chapter 16.

[64]Aric Press and John O'Connor, *Lessons of the Am Law 100*, American Lawyer (May 1, 2007), *available at* **http://www.law.com/jsp/tal/PubArticleTAL.jsp?hubtype=Cover+Story&id=1177578266432**.

[65]Gina Passarella, *Why Qui Tam Practices Work Best at Small Firms*, The Legal Intelligencer (July 10, 2008).

explains, "It's like doing plaintiffs work in a large firm, but because it can garner more publicity and generate pretty significant damages . . . it becomes a little more problematic."[66]

Thus, a lawyer seeking to establish a firm ideally suited to handle a *qui tam* action would need to assess where to find clients, where to locate the firm, how to staff matters, and how to keep the lights on and rent paid during the several years it may take to obtain a return on a *qui tam* action. Such a lawyer would likely want to avoid the plush offices, fine stationery, and other amenities often found at larger corporate-focused law firms.

This section should not be read to suggest that strategic alignment is a concern at all law firms. Most law firms handle any or almost any legal work that a lawyer can generate, particularly if the lawyer or firm believes the client will pay well for the work. Many firms narrow their practice, but often only due to the experience, opportunities, or personal taste of the lawyers, not a conscious strategic decision by the firm or its management. Moreover, firms may narrow their practice but retain other characteristics apparently inconsistent with the narrowed practice. A lawyer may evolve his or her practice to a particular type of law, for example, but retain an office location, paralegals, and other resources more consistent with a prior, non-focused practice rather than with the more limited, focused practice.

While firms may not consciously focus on strategic alignment, considering strategic focus may help a newer lawyer seeking to build his or her own practice. A newer lawyer at an established firm will often find it easiest to develop new work and new clients if the work and clients are essentially aligned with the firm's present systems, clients, and resources. Thus, a lawyer joining a tax firm will likely find it easier to develop some related field, perhaps tax litigation, instead of trying to do something completely different, like practicing equine law or handling speeding tickets.

---

[66]*Id.*

Types of Law Practices

16

Just as there is wide variation in the legal services that clients require, there are wide variations in the types of law firms established to meet those needs. As a preliminary matter, law firms may be divided into three types—traditional "general practice" firms; those firms that primarily seek to deliver legal services to individuals ("consumer-focused firms"); and those firms that target their services to corporate entities, nonprofits, and certain wealthy individuals or families ("corporate-focused firms"). This is a modification of the "two-hemisphere" theory proffered in the 1975 book and study *Chicago Lawyers.* In *Chicago Lawyers*, authors Heinz and Laumann posit that the legal profession can be divided into two hemispheres: those lawyers who serve individuals and those who serve corporations.[67]

For each of these three categories of firms, there are dozens of unique types of firms each with unique

[67]John P. Heinz, Edward O. Laumann, *Chicago Lawyers: The Social Structure of the Bar* (1982). The 1975 study upon which *Chicago Lawyers* was based was refined and conducted a second time in 1995, and this became the focus of John P. Heinz et al., *Urban Lawyers: The New Social Structure of the Bar* (2005).

individual traits. This text, however, deals with only a few examples of consumer-focused and corporate-focused firms. Also, firms that provide transactional, divorce, tax, or similar services to high-net worth individuals may operate in a manner more similar to typical corporate-focused firms than to consumer-focused firms. Consumer- and corporate-focused firms inevitably blend at the edges, and sometimes a consumer-focused firm operates more like a corporate-firm or vice versa.

Traditional General Practice Firms

A traditional general practice firm has one or a few lawyers who provide all types of legal services for clients. In smaller communities (which likely would not have been considered in Heinz and Laumann's study of Chicago lawyers), a lawyer may serve all types of clients on all or virtually all types of legal matters. One rural solo lawyer, for example, represented clients in a multi-million dollar plaintiff's case, divorce, driving while intoxicated, trust and estates, and corporate formation matters, while also serving as back-up county prosecutor when the main prosecutor had a conflict. If a global corporation needed a lawyer in his locality to defend a local lawsuit, he would also likely be considered. After all, only a few years ago, he was one of less than a handful of lawyers who practiced actively in his county.

In larger communities, such general practice firms often find it more difficult to thrive because more focused firms can position themselves to serve potential clients (corporate and consumer clients) and specific legal needs better. Thus, over time such general practice firms tend to migrate their practice to focus on either consumer or corporate clients and toward specific types of matters. As a result, they begin to resemble more the second or third category of firm than a traditional general practice firm.

Consumer-Focused Firms

Consumer-focused firms target consumers as potential clients. They are sometimes also referred to as "retail law firms." They include a broad array of law firms, including firms that represent plaintiffs in lawsuits and people in divorce, criminal, and civil matters including both litigation (for example, commercial disputes, employment or bankruptcy matters) and transactional matters (such as real estate closings, forming corporations, and the like).

While it is somewhat difficult to generalize, consumer-focused firms tend to market themselves more through mainstream media including television and radio advertising, the telephone directories, and the like. Many consumer-focused firms also offer an array of alternative (not time-based) fee arrangements, including contingency fee and fixed fee arrangements. Some lawyers have also found that consumers are interested in value-based billing arrangements. (All these billing arrangements are discussed later in this text.)

Consumer-focused firms also frequently locate new lawyers through different means than corporate-focused firms use. Most are smaller firms—likely a few dozen lawyers at most—and do little on-campus recruiting or hiring of summer associates. Instead, consumer-focused firms likely select candidates for employment from among those people who contact them seeking employment. They also frequently use bar association or other employment opportunity websites to solicit potential employees. Many such firms will expect candidates seeking employment to already have their license in the jurisdiction where they intend to practice. Sometimes such lawyers will also be encouraged to start developing business right away.

Some consumer-focused firms distinguish themselves by handling a large volume of lower-paying work. To make profits off such work, ordinarily the firm's partners vigorously control other costs, including by using lower-cost office space and equipment and lower-cost legal help such as paralegals or low-compensated lawyers. (High leverage becomes common as consumer-focused firms grow.) Also, consumer-focused firms often spend considerably more on marketing than corporate-based firms, and such marketing is the type that would be seen by consumers: television and radio advertisements, billboards, yellow pages advertisements, and the like. Consumer-focused firms may also use and experience greater return from community-service activities, such as sponsoring local festivals or providing emergency or other aid to members of their communities in need.

Examples of typical high-volume consumer-based firms include:

- Traffic law firms
- Personal injury and workers compensation firms
- Basic trust and estate practices
- Consumer bankruptcy firms

Many such firms handle work that is lower down the value pyramid, work that involves more standardized (some call it "commoditized") legal services. But this does not mean that such firms are unprofitable. As discussed above, a firm handling a high-volume of lower-level work may be more profitable than the corporate-focused firms.

Consumer-focused firms may also primarily provide legal services higher on the value pyramid. For example, some consumer-focused firms provide primarily high-value tax, real estate, or litigation services. A few consumer-focused firms even provide services at the very top of the value pyramid, such as the most sophisticated plaintiffs' litigation firms or the highest-level divorce or trust and estate firms.

Corporate-Focused Firms

Corporate-focused firms typically handle legal work for companies (both profit and non-profit entities), and sometimes also for wealthy individuals or families. Corporate-focused firms may provide a very broad or narrow set of legal services. Traditionally, larger corporate law firms sought to provide one-stop shopping to corporate clients. The large firms offered business, tax, litigation, environmental, employment, banking, real estate, white collar defense, and virtually any other type of law that a company might want. Normally such large firms were divided into large practice groups—typically litigation and corporate, plus possibly tax or other practices. But more limited firms, sometimes referred to as boutiques, have also long existed to provide a narrower focus of services to clients. Such firms may provide only litigation, intellectual property, real estate, tax, transactional, or similar services.

The current trend is for even large firms to focus more narrowly on particular types of work or particular types of clients. An example is Howrey, which despite having approximately 700 lawyers is narrowly focusing its practice. In fact, since 2007, Howrey has listed three areas of practice—antitrust, global litigation, and intellectual property—on its website.

Corporate-focused firms tend to limit advertising. They generally avoid television and radio advertisements except perhaps a "tombstone" sponsorship notice on Public Broadcasting System or National Public Radio.[68] Also, their "advertisements" in telephone directories often include little more than the name, address, and telephone number of the firm. Most focus on obtaining work through referrals from existing or former clients, or involvement in bar, civil, or other groups.

Corporate-focused firms often focus on academic credentials when hiring new associates. At least until the 2008 economic downturn, most larger corporate-focused firms tended to employ some form of the Cravath system, selecting junior attorneys in or right after law school, employing them to work on the firm's clients, and subjecting them to a clearer promotion path, including consideration for partnership. Particularly larger corporate-focused firms—which are more able to anticipate client work several years in the future—tended to recruit earlier, often hiring second (or first) year students to serve as summer law clerks or "summer associates." These summer associates would work for and be courted by the firm, and often would receive an offer to return after law school or, for first-year summer associates, the next summer. Such offers might include bar reviews expenses and a summer stipend to help them study for the bar exam. Moreover, while many now offer some form of alternative billing, these firms tend primarily to use time-based fees. The 2008 economic downturn has challenged this model. Some firms are now reducing or eliminating billable hour requirements and reducing pay for newer associates, and using the first-year (or more) at the firm as more of a training period or apprenticeship.

Although corporate-focused firms are often perceived to be more prestigious, they may serve clients at virtually any level of the value chain. Sometimes a corporate-focused firm will take on lower-

[68]A "tombstone advertisement" refers to a simple text advertisement, normally a few lines of black print on a light background and enclosed in a simple box.

value work for a client, perhaps because of the nature of the client, the desire to keep the client happy, or to gain valuable experience and exposure or opportunities for its lawyers. One large Midwestern corporate firm, for example, agreed to handle small-dollar claims for a heavy equipment manufacturer at discounted rates to give its junior litigation associates more experience. Another large corporate-focused firm, New York's Simpson Thatcher & Bartlett, agreed to provide legal services for the Treasury Department's bailout at $300,000 maximum for an estimated 2,632 attorney hours and 1,128 legal assistant hours, or about $114 per attorney hour (with legal assistant hours provided at no charge).[69] Simpson Thatcher likely perceived this engagement would have a *pro bono* component, but also recognized the engagement would provide money and other value to the firm such as experience and positive public relations.

---

[69]*See* Contract between Department of the Treasury and Simpson Thatcher & Bartlett MNP LLP at 5 (Oct. 10, 2008), *available at* **http://amlawdaily.typepad.com/amlawdaily/files/lawfirmcontract.pdf**.

How Fees Are Assessed

17

Law firms use five types of billing arrangements, either in pure or in combination and form: (1) *time-based billing* where the fee is based on the amount of time the lawyer spends on the client's work; (2) *fixed fee billing* where the client pays a particular fee no matter how long the matter takes or what the outcome is; (3) *contingent fees* where the fee is determined by the outcome of the matter, often the amount the client receives (or pays); (4) *asset-based fees* where the fee is determined by the amount of assets managed or handled; and (5) *value-based billing* where the fee is determined based upon the value the client receives.

Time-based billing remains the most prevalent, and is so prevalent that other billing arrangements are sometimes referred to as "alternative billing arrangements." Yet a significant portion of lawyers also offer alternative billing arrangements: a 2007 survey found that 88 percent of respondents offered some form of alternative billing arrangement, primarily fixed fees, contingency fees, and monthly retainers (which are generally just another form of fixed fee).[70] The legal

[70]*See* 2007 ALM Research Report, *Billing Rates and Practices* 3 (2008), *available at* **http://almresearchonline.typepad.com/2007BillingRatesPracticesExecSummary.pdf**. Various types of retainers are discussed in Chapter 25.

media indicates use of alternative billing increased since the 2008 economic downturn.

Fees may also be a mixture of these five methods. For example, firms sometimes represent plaintiff corporations in commercial or IP litigation under an arrangement where the firm charges a (sometimes significantly) discounted hourly rate but also receives a percentage of the total recovery or the recovery above a certain amount. In one case, a large Midwestern firm charged an approximately 30% discount on hourly rates, but received a significant bonus (approximately $3 million) when they defeated class certification, effectively ending the case.

With the exception of statutory fees (where a state or federal statute determines what will be charged or the limits on what can be charged), ordinarily the billing arrangement and fees are established by agreement between the lawyer and client. There is not total freedom of contract, however, because state ethics rules usually impose limits that the fee charged and collected must be neither unreasonable nor unconscionable.[71] This reasonable fee requirement applies to all fee arrangements, including fixed, value, and contingency-fee arrangements.[72]

Time-Based Billing

In the context of time-based billing, the term "rates" normally refers to the rate that a lawyer charges per unit of his or her time. Billing rates at law firms today vary widely: some lawyers—even partners—may bill only $100 or less per hour, while other lawyers may bill $1,000 or more per hour for their time. Factors that influence rates include: the size of a firm, its practice, and environment; the size and maturity of the local market for legal services; and the experience and expertise of the particular lawyer.

Rates are normally quoted on an hourly basis, but are usually charged in smaller increments, ordinarily tenths or quarters of an

[71]*See, e.g.,* ABA Model Rule 1.5(a): "A lawyer shall not make an agreement for, charge, or collect an unreasonable fee or an unreasonable amount for expenses." Model Rule 1.5(a) also lists eight factors that should be considered when determining whether a fee is reasonable.

[72]*See, e.g.*, ABA Model Rule 1.5 cmt [3].

hour. Billing by one-tenth of an hour (six minute) increments is the most common, and is required by many corporate clients to avoid paying .25 hours for a three-minute telephone call. Where the unit of time exceeds an hour or day, it is often perceived to be a fixed-fee engagement.

To give you a sense of rates, in 2007 St. Louis partners at smaller general practice firms or certain types of larger firms (those who offer primarily offer more commoditized services) frequently charged between $150 and $300 per hour. This is consistent with the American Lawyer Media (ALM) 2007 ALM Research Report *Billing Rates and Practices*, which reports the average billing rate nationwide is $240 per hour.[73]

At larger or more specialized firms, however, paralegals may charge $250 per hour (albeit normally for a paralegal supervisor or specialist), while partners may bill clients at rates of $700 or more per hour.

Similar disparities exist nationwide. The 250 or so largest firms, also known as the *National Law Journal (NLJ) 250*, reported median billing rates for 2008 were approximately $350 per hour, up from $347 in 2007.[74] Top partners at some firms now bill $1,000 or more per hour.[75] In 2008, for example, White & Case told the *National Law Journal* that its highest partner rate was $1,120 per hour and its highest associate billing rate was $920 per hour. White & Case reported its average partner rate was $747 per hour and its average associate rate was $456 per hour.[76]

---

[73]*See* 2007 ALM Research Report, *Billing Rates and Practices* 1 (2008), *available at* **http://almresearchonline.typepad.com/2007BillingRatesPracticesExecSummary.pdf**.

[74]Leigh Jones, *Still gaining atmosphere*, National Law Journal (Dec. 10, 2007).

[75]*Id.*; *see also* Debra Cassens Weiss, *Big Firm Hourly Billing Rates Up Almost 8 Percent; Average is $348* (Dec. 11, 2007), *available at* **http://www.abajournal.com/news/big_firm_hourly_billing_rates_up_almost_8_average_is_348/** (reporting top rates at firms including Wilmer Cutler Pickering Hale and Dorr; Simpson Thatcher & Bartlett; Cadwalader, Wickersham & Taft; and Fried, Frank, Harris, Shriver, & Jacobsen exceed $1000 per hour). As of late 2008, the highest billing rate per hour at corporate-focused firms had exceeded $1,200 per hour.

[76]Leigh Jones, *Law Firm Fees Defy Gravity, Annual Survey Shows*, National Law Journal (Dec. 8, 2008) (discussing that White & Case reported its highest rate for partners was $1,260 per hour), *available at* **http://www.law.com/jsp/article.jsp?id=1202426547201**.

Rates tend to be highest in large cities along the coasts and in Chicago: in late 2007, several Los Angeles firms reported median rates above $500.[77] Typically rates are much lower in smaller cities and in the middle of the country. Also, certain practices tend to bill at higher rates than other practices. According to a 2006 Altman Weil study, the highest billing rates were in the following practices:

Non-litigation practices:

Municipal Finance ($395/hour)
Securities ($390/hour)
Mergers and Acquisitions ($375/hour)

Litigation practices:

Antitrust ($420/hour)
Intellectual Property ($388/hour)
Securities ($370/hour)[78]

Firms typically assign rates through one of two systems: a lawyer-based system or a client-based system. In a lawyer-based system, each lawyer has a "standard" billing rate. Clients are then charged that lawyer's standard rate, perhaps with a discount or premium imposed.

Examples for rates may be as follows:

	Standard Rate	Discounted Rate (10% discount)
Employment litigation partner (25 years experience)	$450	$405
Antitrust litigation partner (12 years experience)	$550	$500
Patent litigation associate (9 years experience)	$500	$450
Employment litigation associate (9 years experience)	$300	$270

[77] *Billing Rates at large L.A. firms above the national average* (Dec. 11, 2007), available at **http://www.lalegalpad.com/2007/12/index.html**.

[78] James D. Cotterman, *New Survey Provides Snapshot of Law Firm Economics Across U.S.* (Aug. 2, 2007), *available at* **http://www.altmanweil.com/index.cfm/fa/r.resource_detail/oid/87716caa-56df-4ad9-b375-9e9366ba6d60/resources/New_Survey_Provides_Snapshot_of_Law_Firm_Economics_Across_US.cfm**.

As this chart illustrates, in a lawyer-based system the status of the lawyer as well as the lawyer's experience may not fully determine the relative rate of that lawyer. An associate in one practice may charge more than a senior partner[79] in another practice, even though both are at the same firm.

Under a lawyer-based rate system, firms often expect that every client will pay either the standard or discounted rate for a particular lawyer no matter what services are being performed. Thus, if a client retained the firm for employment litigation, and then involved the services of the patent litigation associate, the client would be expected to pay the regular or discounted rate ($450 or $500 per hour in the chart above) for that patent litigator's work.

Firms that use a lawyer-based system vary in how much they force lawyers to charge their standard rates. Some firms allow lawyers to exercise great flexibility, and tell them to use the standard rates as targets. Other firms, particularly very high-value national firms, direct lawyers to always bill at their standard rate except in exceptional circumstances. At such firms, partners whose clients refuse to pay the standard rates may be asked to terminate the clients or leave the firm. The 2008 economic downturn has created significant pressure on billing rates, often causing even the most disciplined firms to offer discounts.

Under the client-based system, the rate is mainly set by the client, not by the qualifications of the lawyer doing the work. The law firm may have several (often a dozen or more) rate schedules, and assign a client's matter to a particular schedule (perhaps with client-specific modifications) that specifies rates for partners, associates, and paralegals, plus possibly additional rates for subgroups (for example, for junior and senior partners or associates). Alternatively, partners may be given target average rates, but are then left to reach an agreement with particular clients on what rates those clients will pay for each lawyer or type of lawyer's services.

---

[79]Some firms vary billing rates for partners based on whether the partners are equity, non-equity, or contract partners. But firms are more likely to vary rates based upon the experience or expertise of the attorney. In such a firm, the term "senior partner" often refers to a person of particular experience, regardless of whether that person is an equity, non-equity, or contract partner. Likewise, the term "partner" often refers to a person of less experience, regardless of whether that partner is an equity, nonequity, or contract partner.

Sample billing schedules for a client-based system may appear as follows:

	Schedule A	Schedule B	Schedule C
Senior partner	$450	$420	$280
Partner	$400	$420	$230
Senior Attorney	$350	$330	$180
Senior Associate	$300	$280	$150
Junior Associate	$250	$280	$120
Paralegal	$150	$150	$ 90

Under this system, a client pays for each lawyer's time based upon the status of that lawyer (*i.e.*, whether the lawyer is an equity or senior partner, non-equity partner, senior associate, junior associate, and the like).

Under such a system, some clients may pay the same rate for several classes of persons. In this example, Schedule B has only one rate for partners, $420 per hour. Thus, the client agreeing to Schedule B rates would pay $420 per hour for any partner who does work for the client, regardless of practice, experience, reputation, and the like. Also, all associates bill at $280 per hour, regardless of whether those associates are senior or junior associates.

Neither a lawyer-based or client-based system is necessarily better. Lawyer rates, and firm profitability, can vary without regard to which system is used. Additionally, many firms use a mix of lawyer-based and client-based fees. Some firms, for example, will use a lawyer-based system with most clients, but will agree to particular fee schedules for certain clients, perhaps larger or more important clients. Even then, the firm may insist that certain specialists receive fees in excess of the ordinary schedule.

Finally, sometimes the billing rates for all attorneys or for all fee earners (*i.e.*, attorneys and paralegals) at a firm are the same for a client or matter. This type of billing is known as a "blended rate." For example, a client may agree to pay $220 per hour for each hour of work, regardless of who performs the work. Such blended rates are primarily used by large corporations or insurance companies for work they want accomplished very efficiently. Firms operating under such blended rates normally work hard to make sure that the paralegals and the lowest-seniority lawyers do the largest share of work possible on blended-rate matters.

Firms and clients also vary regarding what constitutes billable time. Either by practice or client agreement, some firms do not charge for travel time, unless they are engaged in substantive work on the case during that time (for example, preparing documents or reviewing records while traveling by plane). Sometimes clients will not pay for multiple lawyers to review the same correspondence, or for lawyers to confer with other lawyers within the firm.

While most of these matters are left up to the lawyer and client, ethical rules typically impose certain limitations. As noted above, ordinarily the fees must ultimately be reasonable. ABA Formal Ethics Opinion 93-379 (1993), which has been adopted in a number of jurisdictions, makes clear that under time-based billing arrangements, a lawyer may not bill multiple clients for the same time unless there are separate agreements. Thus, if a lawyer takes a 2-hour flight for client A, and does work for client B while on the flight, the total amount that the lawyer can bill to client A and client B combined may not exceed 2 hours.

ABA Formal Ethics Opinion 93-379 also directs that a lawyer may not bill a client more than the time actually spent on that client's work, even if the client benefits from work the lawyer did for someone else. If the lawyer spends 10 hours on a memorandum for client A and charges client A for that time, and only 1 hour updating that memorandum for client B, the most the lawyer can bill client B is the 1 hour.

Three major criticisms of time-based fees are that (1) they reward inefficient legal work, (2) they encourage dishonest billing, and (3) they create significant strains on lawyers and thwart efforts to improve work-life balance. Time-based billing rewards inefficiency because the lawyer is paid for time spent, not for result. A lawyer who spends 10 minutes to find the perfect solution bills less than the lawyer who spends 10 hours but finds no solution. Also, time-based billing creates an incentive for lawyers to spend more time on a matter, and a less ethical lawyer can almost always justify taking one more deposition or discussing or reviewing a document one more time (a practice often called "churning a file").

Time-based billing encourages dishonest billing because lawyers set their fee based upon the time they spend, and it is almost impossible for anyone—including the client—to verify how much time is spent on a matter. A lawyer may bill hundreds of matters per month; increasing each of those entries by .1 hour (which may suggest only three or four more minutes of additional time per entry) would likely cause the lawyer to increase monthly billings by 20 to 30 hours or more. Concerns with fraud are heightened at firms that require a significant number of hours billed or compensate lawyers based upon the number of hours they bill. Such compensation systems are common: many firms award bonuses of thousands or tens of thousands of dollars for every 100 or 150 hours the lawyer bills in excess of a minimum target (which is often between 1,800 and 2,000 hours).

Finally, the need to bill hours increases the strain on lawyers and their personal lives. A lawyer billing hours is never rewarded for efficiency. Also, a perceived need to bill hours often causes a lawyer to work during what would otherwise be downtime (weekends, holidays, vacation, etc.), or to return to work in circumstances (after significant successes or time away from work) when people not feeling pressure to bill hours might take the rest of the day off, for example.

Nevertheless, time-based billing remains quite common. It provides an easy-to-quantify measurement of work performed. It also protects lawyers from uncertainty regarding how long a matter will take.

Fixed (Flat) Fee Billing

Fixed fee or flat fee billing is any type of billing where the amount billed is set by the unit of production. Examples include:

- An agreement to charge $1,000 to prepare a loan document.
- An agreement to charge $50,000 to litigate a case.
- An agreement to charge $10,000 to serve as outside general counsel for a corporate client.

Note that for each of these examples, the lawyer will earn the agreed fee regardless of how long the project takes or who exactly does the legal work. Thus, if a firm agrees to prepare a loan document for $1,000, the firm may then have a competent associate do all the work on the matter and still collect the $1,000 (presuming supervisory duties imposed for example by ABA Model Rule 5.1 are satisfied). The firm could also bring in experts to handle particular parts of the matter, without worrying that the client might think that using such experts is an effort to increase the bill. Furthermore, as long as the fee was reasonable, the firm could charge $1,000 to both client A and B, even if the firm spends 10 hours preparing the document for client A, and 1 hour modifying it for client B.

Although at one time lawyers claimed that certain types of work could not be done on a fixed fee, the use of fixed fees continues to grow, even for matters like litigation. Sometimes this is accomplished by charging a fixed fee for each unit of work: for example, $3,000 to prepare and argue certain types of motions, or $2,000 plus travel expenses to take a deposition. Clients like fixed-fee billing because it provides greater (or absolute) certainty in legal fees. Lawyers like fixed fee billing because it rewards efficiency and reduces disputes over bills.

Unfortunately, fixed-fee arrangements also create potential problems. Some lawyers use fixed fees in an attempt to earn excessive fees, likely in violation of Rule 1.5. Some also worry that fixed fees encourage lawyers to delegate work too much or to do too little on a matter, so that the lawyer's profits can be greater. A lawyer's work ethic and the lawyer-client relationship may also suffer when a lawyer determines that he or she is spending much more time and effort to complete a matter than the lawyer anticipated when he or she agreed to complete the matter for an ultimately inadequate fixed fee. Finally, particularly for lawyers who typically bill by the hour, it may seem unfair to charge a client a particular fee when the matter takes less time than expected, or to charge two clients the same amount when the work takes much longer for one client than the other.

Contingent Fees

Contingent fees broadly defined include any billing arrangement where the fee that will be charged is dependent upon the outcome of the matter. The prototypical contingency fee is that used in a personal injury case. A plaintiff's lawyer may agree to receive one-third or one-quarter (or more) of a plaintiff's recovery, and then handle the representation often without other compensation. More often, the contingency fee in a personal injury case will vary depending upon the amount of work performed. For example, a contingency fee agreement may provide that the plaintiff's lawyer will receive 25 percent of any settlement received before trial, 33 percent of any settlement or judgment received during trial, or 40 percent of any settlement or judgment received after trial, including on appeal.

Contingency fees may be used in almost any type of case, not just personal injury matters, with the exception of criminal defense cases and certain types of family law matters where ethics rules may prohibit contingency fees.[80] Contingency fees may be used for defending civil cases (where the firm receives a particular fee or specified bonus if the matter is dismissed or resolved for less than a specified amount), or for selling a home or business, or for completing financing for a business deal.[81]

Further, a contingent fee is not necessarily a percentage fee. The key aspect of a contingency fee is that payment is contingent upon the happening of some event. Thus, a contingent fee exists in each of the following situations:

- The lawyer and client agree that, if the lawyer obtains dismissal of the case within 90 days, the lawyer will receive a $1000 bonus.
- The lawyer and client agree the lawyer will prepare a will for $1500, and receive a $1000 bonus if the will is not successfully contested.
- The lawyer and client agree the lawyer will receive $1000 for legal work on a business deal, or $2,500 if the transaction closes.

Contingency fees tend to be subject to more stringent regulation than some other types of billing arrangements. Generally contingency fee agreements must be in writing, and the writing must

---

[80]*See* ABA Model Rule 1.5(d), which states, "A lawyer shall not enter into an arrangement for, charge, or collect: (1) any fee in a domestic relations matter, the payment or amount of which is contingent upon the securing of a divorce or upon the amount of alimony or support, or property settlement in lieu thereof; or (2) a contingent fee for representing a defendant in a criminal case."

[81]One noted example of this is the fee Cravath Swain & Moore received for its work on the Time-Warner merger.

clearly state how the fee will be calculated, including whether expenses will be deducted before or after the fee is calculated. ABA Model Rule 1.5(c) states in part:

> A contingent fee agreement shall be in a writing signed by the client and shall state the method by which the fee is to be determined, including the percentage or percentages that shall accrue to the lawyer in the event of settlement, trial or appeal; litigation and other expenses to be deducted from the recovery; and whether such expenses are to be deducted before or after the contingent fee is calculated. The agreement must clearly notify the client of any expenses for which the client will be liable whether or not the client is the prevailing party.

Contingency fees also face criticism, and may be struck down, if they fail to reflect when the lawyer is likely incurring little risk when accepting the representation, or if the percentage of recovery sought is deemed excessive in light of what legal services the client will receive.

Treatment of costs is often an issue in contingency fee cases. First, the lawyer and client often must establish whether the lawyer or client will pay third-party expenses (such as expert fees, filing fees, and litigation-related costs such as depositions and the like) if the client obtains no recovery through the matter.[82] Second, if recovery is obtained, the lawyer and client need to resolve whether the lawyer's fee will be a percentage of the gross recovery, or a percentage of the net recovery after expenses are deducted. This can be a major consideration. If the client recovers $100,000, but has incurred $50,000 in expenses obtaining that recovery, a lawyer receiving 25 percent of the recovery would receive $25,000 if the fee were calculated before expenses were deducted, but only $12,500 if the fee were calculated after the expenses were deducted. If a lawyer and client do not reach an agreement on the handling of costs, courts will ordinarily require the lawyer and client to share in paying costs, and thus allow the lawyer to take his or her fee only after costs have been deducted

---

[82]*See* ABA Model Rule 1.8(e), which permits a client's payment of costs and expenses to be contingent upon their recovery in a matter.

from the full recovery. Some states require that expenses be deducted before the lawyer's fee is calculated.

Contingency fees are often criticized because they may allow a lawyer to receive a very large fee for doing very little work. For example, if a lawyer is fortunate enough to represent a seriously injured individual where liability is almost certain, a lawyer may receive a $10 million settlement, and thus a $3 or $4 million fee, simply by sending a letter. Also, a lawyer being paid on contingency may be motivated to settle a case quickly and with little effort, instead of working harder and possibly gaining a larger settlement for his or her client. Finally, lawyers being paid on contingency have incentive to seek settlements in virtually any case, including cases that have little or no merit.

Contingency fees may also create problems for the lawyer-client relationship. Clients do not like when a lawyer receives a significant portion of a settlement with little or no effort, particularly if the large settlement is due to the client's severe injuries (and not the lawyer's diligent and competent representation). Clients also may not fully understand the impact of having the lawyer's fee deducted before expenses are paid. In our prior example, the lawyer had a 25 percent contingency fee, expenses were $50,000, and total recovery was $100,000. If the lawyer's fee is deducted before the expenses are paid, the lawyer and client would each ultimately receive $25,000. A client who expects to receive three times more than his or her lawyer may perceive such a result as unfair.

Differing expectations on the outcome of a matter can also create major problems in contingency fee representations. For example, a client who has unreal expectations regarding the outcome of a matter may decide to ignore a lawyer's recommendation and force the lawyer to sink more time (and money) into a matter when the lawyer does not expect to make a recovery that would justify the time and expenses.

Asset-Based Fees

Asset-based fees are fees that are assessed based upon the value of assets. Often such a fee is used for financial services: lawyers may charge a fee based upon the amount of assets under management. Asset-based fees are also used for real-estate closing services. A lawyer may charge one amount for properties less than a certain threshold, and more for more valuable properties.

Asset fees are a bit of a hybrid: they share many aspects of fixed fees, but fluctuate (and thus are somewhat contingent upon) the value of the assets. Asset-based fees are also not very common in the legal industry.

Value-Based Billing

In true or pure value-based billing, the lawyer negotiates the fee based upon the value the client places upon the matter or outcome of the matter. This may involve a negotiation of the fee after the matter is over, based upon the value the matter brought to the client. The focus is not how long the lawyer worked or how much the lawyer did, but the value or benefit the client received.

Employing value-based billing usually requires the lawyer and client to discuss, agree upon, and document the goals of the representation at the start of the representation, and to discuss how valuable reaching those goals would be. The lawyer then has parallel interests with the client in trying to obtain those goals, and is usually compensated based upon the extent to which the client's goals were reached.

In true value-based billing, the amount of the fee can be seen as "extremely arbitrary and judgmental. There is no standard markup to the usual rate, no contingency arrangement based upon a certain result, nor a bonus added to the agreed upon price. Fees are based on the time it takes to solve a problem, complexity of situation and the amount at stake—all of which are intangible components."[83] For this reason, value-based billing can sometimes be hard to implement: clients may be concerned such billing is a tool for a lawyer to gouge the client.

---

[83]Tara Teichgraeber, *Value-based billing still difficult to implement*, The Business Journal of Phoenix (Oct. 15, 1999), *available at* **http://www.bizjournals.com/phoenix/stories/1999/10/18/focus2.html.**

This description of value-based billing is quite narrow. Sometimes lawyers or those commenting on the legal industry use the term "value-based billing" to refer to a matter where the fee is negotiated at the outset, based upon the importance of the matter to the client. One such instance is where the lawyer and client agree upon a significant fee, such as a $1 million fee to handle a piece of litigation, because that representation is very important to the client. For our purposes, however, this is not true value billing. It is a fixed-fee engagement.

Also, sometimes lawyers or legal industry commentators use value billing to describe an arrangement where compensation is based upon accomplishing pre-determined objectives, with fixed amounts paid for each objective achieved. For example, the lawyer and client may agree that the lawyer will receive one fee if a business deal is completed, another if it is not. This is also not true value billing; it is a contingent-fee engagement.

Each of these representations shares some characteristics with value billing, including that the fee charged is based upon the value the client places on the matter or the outcome. However, each is more properly categorized as another type of billing—fixed- or contingency-fee billing. When such examples are excluded from value billing, what remains are those representations where the lawyer and client resolve the fee only upon determining exactly what value the client derives. This normally can be accomplished only at the end of the representation.

Noted Hybrid Arrangements

While some smaller firms use a wide variety of billing arrangements, many large firms remain anchored to time-based (hourly) billing. Some of the most noted corporate-focused firms, however, have largely moved away from hourly billing to alternative billing arrangements. Two of these firms have achieved enough notoriety—Bartlit Beck and Wachtell Lipton—that this section describes their billing methods briefly.

The firm selected as *American Lawyer*'s litigation boutique of 2008, Chicago's Bartlit Beck Herman Palenchar & Scott LLP, typically uses a monthly fee arrangement with a contingent component. *American Lawyer* described Bartlit Beck's typically billing arrangements as follows:

> The firm negotiates its compensation individually with each client, but typically clients pay a flat monthly fee, holding back a percentage ranging from 20 percent to 40 percent. If the case goes awry, the client pockets the holdback. If the client wins, the firm receives a bonus that can amount to five times the holdback or more.[84]

While many corporate-focused firms claim they cannot abandon hourly billing, Bartlit Beck has apparently not submitted an hourly bill to a client in years. The firm even claims to turn down work from clients too wedded to hourly billing.[85]

New York's Wachtell, Lipton, Rosen & Katz, frequently the most profitable firm listed on the *Am Law 100*, also generally eschews hourly billing. Its typical billing method on its most prevalent work, merger and acquisition work, is a fee based upon a percentage of the transactions on which it works. According to the *American Lawyer*, a 2001 memorandum that Wachtell Lipton gave to prospective clients stated that the firm typically bases its bills not on the time the lawyers spend, but on the "complexity of the transaction, the intensity of the firm's efforts, and the results achieved." As of 2001, this often amounted to 1% of the value of a transaction valued at less than $100 million, 0.25% of the overall value of a transaction valued at $1 billion, or 0.10% of a transaction valued at more than $20 billion.[86] Thus, Wachtell Lipton used a billing system akin to asset-based billing.

---

[84]David Bario, *Litigation Boutique of the Year Winner: Bartlit Beck*, American Lawyer (Jan. 5, 2009).

[85]*Id.*

[86]Douglas McCollam, *Wachtell's Secret Formula,* American Lawyer (Oct. 2001).

18 Other Sources of Firm Revenue

In addition to billing for legal services provided, some law firms generate revenues through a variety of other services. Most of these revenue sources are similar to revenue that might be generated by other types of businesses. For example, a law firms may generate revenue by subleasing rented unneeded space to a subtenant.

There are two types of non-fee revenue that may create special issues or opportunities for law firms. First, some firms sell law-related services, services that often appear similar to legal services but can be performed by lawyers and nonlawyers alike. Examples include advising or training on law-related issues such as business, bankruptcy, environmental compliance, government relations, human resources, or virtually any other law-related field, as well as providing lobbying, title insurance, trust management, or similar services. A law firm may provide these services through a related entity that operates largely freed from the ethical rules that govern the provision of legal services,[87] or the firm may provide such services as part of the firm's ordinary operations. Law firms of all sizes use both approaches to supplement the income they generate from practicing law.

Second, some firms generate revenue by seeking premiums from clients. Often the possibility of a premium is raised at the outset of a representation, typically in an engagement letter. Then the lawyer will seek to obtain such a premium from the client after the matter is resolved by emphasizing the success obtained and requesting some amount over ordinary amounts billed. Clients sometimes agree to pay such premiums.[88] A *New York Times* article suggests that requests from major New York corporate firms for premiums of 25 to 30 percent of hourly billings were not uncommon for merger and acquisition work during the boom of the late 1990s and early 2000s.[89]

Sometimes either contingent payments or value-based billing are called "premiums" or confused with premiums. For purposes of this text, if all or a portion of fees are left open until the value of the representation can be determined, this is value-based billing. If the lawyer can earn a definite right to an extra payment by satisfying some condition, this is a contingent fee arrangement. A premium is different in that the lawyer has no real right or expectation to such payment. A premium payment occurs when, either at the request of the lawyer or on its own initiative, a grateful client pays a lawyer a larger fee than was originally negotiated between the lawyer and client.

---

[87]ABA Model Rule 5.7 provides certain guidelines when a lawyer may operate a law-related business and not comply with ethical rules that normally govern the provision of legal services. Advantages typically sought by law-related businesses include allowing nonlawyers to share in the ownership of the law-related business, and advertising or soliciting clients in ways that cannot be used to solicit clients for legal services. But clients of such separate businesses do not gain all the protections of a lawyer-client relationship, including fiduciary duties and application of the lawyer-client privilege to communications related to the law-related services.

[88]Apparently sometimes law firms also include premiums on bills without client notice and approval. Ethical rules generally do not permit such practices.

[89]David Lat, *When $1,000 an Hour Is Not Enough*, New York Times (Oct. 3, 2007).

Law Firm Profitability

19

Basics of Firm Profitability

There are five levers to law firm profitability: rates, utilization, leverage, expenses, and speed (which can easily be remembered through the acronym "RULES").[90] Each of these five levers has an impact on the profitability of the firm. No single lever is more important than the other, although some may be easier to change to increase revenues or profitability.

Rates

Rates are the level at which a lawyer bills for his or her services. Regardless of whether the fees are time-based, fixed, or contingency billing, the lawyer must determine how much a service or unit of service will cost. Will the client pay $400 per hour or $200? Will the client pay $3,000 for testamentary documents or $1,000? Will the client pay a 33 percent or 40 percent contingency? A law firm can increase profits by increasing its rates.

---

[90]Stephen Mayson, *Making Sense of Law Firms* 412 (2006).

An increase in rates, however, may impact other profitability factors, in particular utilization, because clients may leave a law firm if rates increase. Recognizing that limits exist on rates, firms will often try to increase the "realized" rates even if they cannot raise their nominal (or stated) rates. Realization refers to the percent of fees billed that are actually collected. Realized rates are increased whenever the amount that is "realized" or collected from the clients is increased. Under ordinary circumstances, a client may receive a reduction either at the outset of a matter, when the lawyer agrees to a lower rate, or at some subsequent time, including when the client requests a discount, or the billing lawyer writes off part of the bill because the lawyer believes the amount billed would be excessive or the client cannot or will not pay. A firm can increase its realized rate, and thus its profitability, by decreasing such discounting or writing down of bills.

Prior to the 2008 economic downturn, it was not uncommon for firms to have realization rates in excess of 90 percent. This would include premiums, which could cause realization for a particular matter to exceed 100 percent. The 2008 economic downturn has caused many firms to suffer severe drops in their realization rates.

Utilization

Utilization refers to how much the resources of an entity are put to productive use. For a law firm, this generally means how much output or client work the fee earners—mainly the lawyers and paralegals—generate. For firms that use time-based billing, it is the measure of how many hours those lawyers and paralegals actually bill. For other firms, it may be the amount that lawyers and paralegals prepare documents, work on cases, or the like.

High utilization requires that the law firm have client work available, as well as people who can and do perform the client work. Thus, there are several limits on utilization. First, the people who can perform the work must also tend to other needs, such as eating and sleeping. Second, someone at the firm must be generating client work, usually through marketing or business development, and also making sure that the firm tends to necessary activities such as paying its bills, providing necessary training and oversight, and the like.

While utilization is not simply about the number of hours billed, the amount of time billed can be a major determinant in the profitability of a lawyer and of a firm. A lawyer who bills 2,000 hours will be more profitable than one who bills 1,900, presuming the additional fees generated for those hours are realized (*i.e.*, collected from the client).

The following diagram illustrates an associate who bills $200 an hour, whose compensation and benefits equal $180,000, and whose overhead allocation (or share of overhead expenses including staff salaries, rent, and the like) equal $100,000. Note that the lawyer must work 900 hours to pay his or her own compensation and benefits, and 1,400 hours before he or she also covers overhead expenses allocated to him or her and breaks even. (The break-even point is 1,400 hours or $280,000 in total revenue realized.) Because there are generally few variable expenses incurred when a salaried lawyer bills additional hours, every hour billed above 1,400 constitutes almost pure profit for the firm.

Billing Break-Even Point

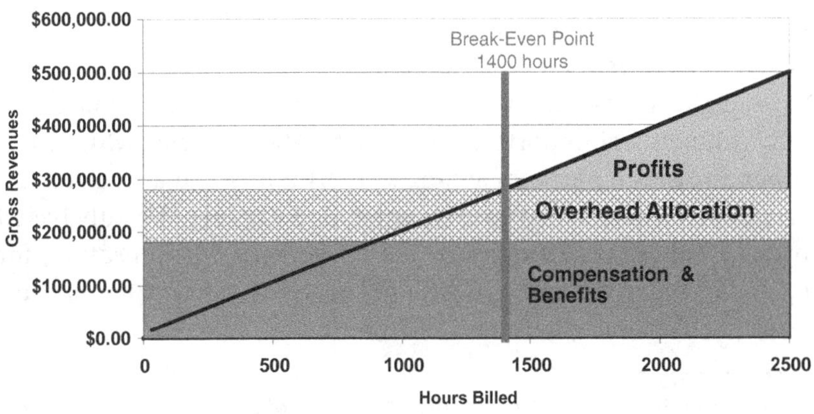

This diagram also illustrates why, as discussed later, firms often pay bonuses to associates that exceed a certain number of billable hours. The firm is sharing part of the profits the associate is generating with the associate. The firm would not pay a bonus on the hours billed up to 1,400, because there is no profit—and no additional funds available to pay a bonus—generated from those hours. The firm then generally wants to retain some profit from the associate's work: this is a benefit that having an associate confers on the firm's partners (they make money off the associate), and also reflects that the partners are generally providing work for the associate to do and taking the risks associated with operating the firm. But at some point the partners received what they consider a reasonable return on the associate. After that point, the partners may be willing to share the profits the associate is generating with the associate.

According to an Altman Weil survey, equity partners in law firms billed a median 1,704 hours in 2006, and associates billed 1,840 hours. For firms with more than 150 lawyers, these medians rose to 1,735 for equity partners and 1,901 hours for associates. Smaller firms with between 9 and 20 lawyers usually billed less: median hours billed were 1,566 for equity partners and 1,700 hours for associates.[91] This may reflect work-life balance choices by the lawyers at such firms, but it also may reflect that lawyers at smaller firms likely need to spend more time running their firms, originating new business, and the like. However, lawyers with management responsibility bill almost as much as lawyers without such responsibilities. According to Altman Weil, "partners with significant management responsibilities in their firms billed only 10% fewer hours than their non-manager peers."[92]

ALM reports hours billed at levels very similar numbers to what Altman Weil reports. According to ALM, at firms with 170 or fewer attorneys, partners averaged 1,701 hours and associates averaged 1,755 hours.[93] Average hours billed vary significantly based upon practice. Litigation partners in workers compensation, for example, bill a median 2,079 hours per year, while trust and estates partners bill a median 1,507 hours.[94]

---

[91] James D. Cotterman, *New Survey Provides Snapshot of Law Firm Economics Across U.S.* (Aug. 2, 2007).

[92] *Id.*

[93] *See* 2007 ALM Research Report, *Billing Rates and Practices* 2 (2008), *available at* **http://almresearchonline.typepad.com/2007BillingRatesPracticesExecSummary.pdf**.

[94] *Id.*

Leverage

Leverage references the ratio of partners—either all partners or just equity partners—to some other group of fee earners at a firm. The most common use of the term—and the ratio to which "leverage" often refers when not explained—is the ratio of partners to non-partner lawyers at the firm. But leverage may also refer to the ratio of equity partners to all fee earners who are not equity partners (which would include all lawyers and nonlawyer billers such as paralegals and specialists), or some other ratio between partners and other lawyers at the firm.

Leverage is important because law firm equity partners generally derive some of their income from the profits generated by lawyers who are not equity partners at the firm. Without leverage, an equity partner would be limited to the profits that he or she could generate. If an equity partner at a large corporate firm billed 2,000 hours at $400 per hour and collected all fees billed, the equity partner's gross revenues would be $800,000. If the overhead attributed to that equity partner was $150,000, the most the equity partner could make in profits from his or her own work is $650,000.

Equity Partner Profits

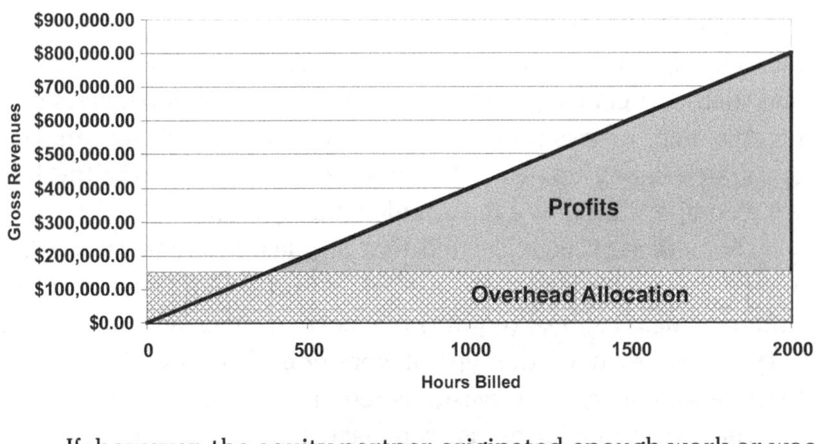

If, however, the equity partner originated enough work or was otherwise entitled to profits generated by other lawyers at the firm, the equity partner could supplement his or her own share of profits with the profits generated by the other lawyer. For example, if the equity partner originated work done by three other associates, each of whom billed 2,000 hours at $200 and generated $120,000 in profits for the firm each year (the same figures used in "Utilization" diagram on the previous page), the partner might be entitled to claim some or all of the $360,000 in additional profits those associates generated. Each associate would generate profits as follows:

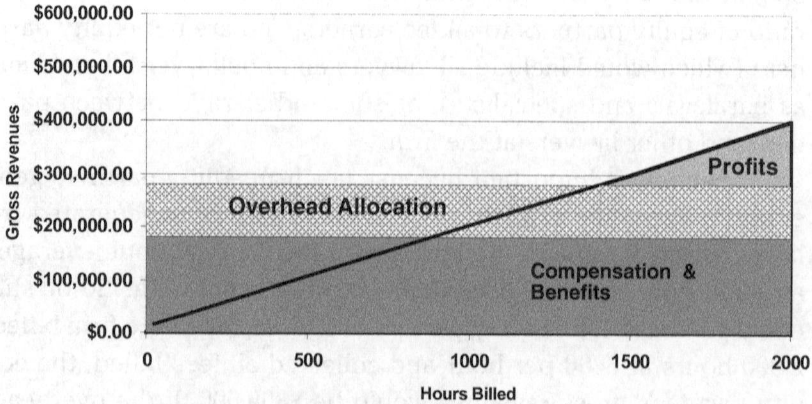

The partner providing the associates with work would expect to receive a portion of each associate's profits. The more associates the partner employed, the greater the amount of profits the partner could hope to share.

At an "eat what you kill firm" (discussed below), the equity partner might in fact receive all or almost all the profits that they and their associates generate. At other firms, equity partners may receive more or less than the profits their work and workers generate, depending upon what system was used and how the lawyer's compensation was fixed under that system.

Sometimes it is suggested that an ideal leverage ratio exists for law firms. This is not the case for all firms—or all lawyers. For a firm, the ideal ratio of (equity) partners to other fee earners will vary depending upon the type of work done. The key will be to determine what level of fee earner is required to perform client work, and the profits that fee earner can make. For example, if a firm does more sophisticated work (higher up the value pyramid), it may benefit from having more senior lawyers and fewer junior lawyers because the more senior lawyers would be required to complete the client's work. (In those circumstances, too many junior lawyers might result in lawyers without enough to do, and thus with low utilization.) If a firm's sole practice is to provide divorce or trust and estate services to high net worth individuals, for example, the firm would likely not benefit greatly from having lots of inexperienced lawyers. Clients would not want to have junior lawyers working on their divorce or their estate. For similar reasons, Wachtell, Lipton, Rosen, & Katz is among the most profitable large firms in the United States,[95] but it has very low leverage—approximately 76 partners to 122 associates, or only about 1:1.6. Wachtell proudly advertises this point on its website, stating: "We operate with a ratio of partners to associates far above that of our major competitors, and matters undertaken by our firm are afforded the direct personal attention of partners having expertise and sophistication with respect to the issues."[96] Similarly, as of January 2009, corporate-focused litigation boutique Bartlit Beck reportedly had 52 partners but only 17 associates, or a partner-associate ratio of 1:0.3.[97]

A firm that primarily handles cases lower on the value pyramid may benefit most from having a much higher leverage ratio. For example, a firm that handles primarily small workers compensation or bankruptcy cases may operate most profitably if it uses a large number of paralegals and junior attorneys to handle such cases. For example, a partner at an insurance defense firm may only be able to bill at $200 per hour. On his or her own, even working 2,500 hours per year, that partner might only generate gross revenue of $500,000, and perhaps profits of $400,000 (the insurance defense firm will likely have lower overhead as well as rates). If this partner's practice can employ a number of associates and paralegals, each of whom generates $75,000 or $50,000 in profits respectively, and keeps each of those people busy, the result may

---

[95]Wachtell's profits per equity partner have exceeded $3 million since 2004. Vivia Chen, *Behind the Numbers*, American Lawyer (March 30, 2007), *available at* **http://www.law.com/jsp/tal/PubArticleTAL.jsp?hubtype=Cover+Story&id=1177578266432**.

[96]*About the Firm*, Wachtell Lipton website, *available at* **http://www.wlrk.com/Page.cfm/Thread/The%20Firm** (visited January 2009).

[97]David Bario, *Litigation Boutique of the Year Winner: Bartlit Beck*, American Lawyer (Jan. 5, 2009).

be profits for the equity partner at the insurance defense firm that rival or exceed those for the equity partner at the large corporate firm described above. The key for the insurance defense firm is to determine what the proper leverage is for its practice.

Leverage works effectively the same way at firms that do not primarily use time-based billing. A Midwestern plaintiffs' firm, for example, has between 50 and 60 staff, and more than 20 attorneys, but only two equity partners. Each of those equity partners made approximately $2 million in 2005, just shy of the profits per equity partner that Wachtell reported for the same period, by having the more junior lawyer and staff handle and resolve contingency-fee matters.

Leverage at larger, corporate-focused firms is often a ratio of 1:3 or 1:4 for equity partners compared to other attorneys. Bryan Cave, for example, had 179 equity partners and 597 other attorneys, or a ratio of about 1 equity partner per 3.3 other attorneys. Before its merger with Hughes & Luce, K&L Gates had 313 equity partners and 1077 other attorneys, or about 1 equity partner per 3.4 other attorneys.[98]

Prior to the 2008 economic downturn, the general trend at the nation's largest firm had been for leverage to increase. This increase was driven primarily by growth in the number of non-equity partners, senior attorneys, and similar non-partner, non-associates. Professor William Henderson of the University of Indiana-Bloomington School of Law found that the total number of lawyers at the *NLJ 250* firms increased by 77 percent (from 56,239 to 99,652) from 1995-2005. The number of associates increased at almost the same rate, by 78 percent. The number of partners, however, increased by only 64.2 percent. Thus, increased leverage was largely a result of non-partner, non-associates (i.e., senior attorneys) joining such firms. Moreover, rate of increase in the number of equity partners at the *NLJ 250* firms increased slower than rate of increase for other partners and associates at such firms from 1995 to 2005. The number of equity partners increased by only

---

[98]*See* Brenda Sapino Jeffreys, *K&L Gates and Hughes & Luce Vote to Combine*, Texas Lawyer (Dec. 18, 2007), *available at* **http://www.law.com/jsp/llf/PubArticleLLF.jsp?id=1197980086541**.

31.7 percent, while the number of non-equity partners increased by 234 percent (from 2,600 to 8,500). Some assert that this large disparity in growth rate between categories of lawyers reflects the importance of the "profits per equity partner" profitability measure, the measure used to rank firms on the *American Lawyer*'s list of the 100 most profitable corporate-focused firms (which list is referred to as the *Am Law 100*).[99] Many top firms have reduced equity partners through demotion or firings in recent years; some blame this on firms' desires to move up the *Am Law 100.*[100]

Finally, a desire to maintain leverage will cause exponential growth of a law firm. If a firm has two equity partners and six associates, it has leverage of equity partners: associates of 1:3. If the firm promotes an associate to equity partner, it would now have three equity partners and five associates. To return to a 1:3 equity partner: associate ratio, the firm would need to hire four more associates. Thus, the eight-lawyer firm would need to grow to twelve to keep the same leverage ratio after promoting one associate to partner. If a lawyer were promoted at a firm that had 1:6 leverage, meanwhile, the firm would need to hire seven more lawyers to keep the desired leverage upon promoting the one lawyer. The result is that law firms have significant growth pressure, and will often increase size rapidly.

Expenses

Expenses refer to the amount of expenses incurred by the firm and not passed onto clients. Depending upon what is billed to a client,

---

[99]The *American Lawyer* publishes a list of the largest and most profitable firms annually, usually in its May edition. In 2006, 59 of the firms had profits per equity in excess of $1 million. The highest profits per equity partner were $4.4 million at Wiley Rein. *See* Vivia Chen, *Behind the Numbers*, American Lawyer (March 30, 2007), *available at* **http://www.law.com/jsp/tal/PubArticleTAL.jsp?hubtype=Cover+Story&id=1177578266432**. This list does not include the most profitable consumer-focused firms, thus ignoring for example the most profitable plaintiffs' firms who in a given year may make much more per equity partner than corporate-based firms.

[100]"Of the 28 firms that posted profits per equity partner increases of 15 percent or more in 2006, 15 had a decrease in the number of equity partners." *Id.*

expenses may range from salaries (for everyone other than equity partners) and rent—normally among the largest expenses for law firms[101]—to continuing education, marketing, and advertising, professional dues, charitable contributions, professional liability and other insurance, and even the cost of computers, stationery, pens, electricity, photocopies and faxes, heat, and air conditioning.

Generally, overhead expenses (including the salaries of non-billing assistants and others, but excluding lawyer and other billing employee salaries) usually total at least $70,000 per lawyer at law firms that have offices. At larger firms, overhead expenses may total $200,000 per lawyer.[102] Likewise, for firms where lawyers work from home and essentially without assistants, overhead expenses may be considerably lower.

Firms can increase their profitability by decreasing the expenses they pay. Firms often do this by adopting strict controls on expenses. For example, a firm may strictly regulate travel for continuing education or client development, when the travel expenses cannot be passed onto clients. Law firms may also decrease the expenses that impact their profitability by increasing the expenses they pass onto clients. Having expenses paid by a client, instead of by the firm, will help the law firm increase its profitability. Expenses passed onto clients include everything from copying or scanning charges (both inside the firm and from outside vendors), transportation costs, filing fees, food, long distance, and sometimes even staff overtime. Often, lawyers and clients agree at the outset about what may or may not be charged to the client as expenses, and more sophisticated clients often have outside counsel guidelines that specify expenses that they will not pay.

---

[101]Writing primarily about the English legal profession, Stephen Mayson estimates that staff costs are usually about 50 percent of expenses, while premises costs including rent are approximately 15 percent of expenses. Stephen Mayson, *Making Sense of Law Firms* 418 (2006).

[102]Altman Weil, *Survey reports that U.S. law firm profits up despite uncertain economy* (July 8, 2003), *available at* **http://www.altmanweil.com/index.cfm/fa/r.resource_detail/oid/27510f49-fc27-45b0-bca0-63eb04ca9aef/resource/Law_Firm_Profits_Up_Despite_Uncertain_Economy_Survey_Reports.cfm**. In the early 2000s, expenses consistently rose at the largest firms. A common impact of the downturn has been that firms have worked hard to control and reduce non-reimbursable costs.

Lawyers and clients exercise considerable freedom of contract on what expenses are paid by clients, but ethics rules and opinions make clear that expenses are not supposed to generate profits for a law firm. A firm may charge for costs it incurred, including a reasonable estimate of overhead incurred when the firm keeps copying, scanning, or similar services in-house. The ABA and many ethics opinions also allow a law firm to impose a reasonable surcharge on third-party costs it seeks to collect, as long as that surcharge is a reasonable estimation of the costs the firm incurs in dealing with that third-party expense (e.g., to account for charges incurred in administering the third-party fee.) The ABA has made clear, however, that law firms should not seek to create secret profit centers by over-billing for expenses. ABA Opinion 93-379 states:

> [I]n the absence of disclosure to the contrary, it would be improper if the lawyer assessed a surcharge on . . . [expense] disbursements over and above the amount actually incurred unless the lawyer herself incurred additional expenses beyond the actual cost of the disbursement item. In the same regard, if a lawyer receives a discounted rate from a third-party provider, it would be improper if she did not pass along the benefit of the discount to her client rather than charge the client the full rate and reserve the profit to herself. Clients quite properly could view these practices as an attempt to create additional undisclosed profit centers when the client had been told he would be billed for disbursements.[103]

Some jurisdictions are more strict than ABA opinion 93-379 and prohibit surcharges unless they are plainly disclosed to clients. To my knowledge, no jurisdiction allows lawyers to add an undisclosed surcharge to an expense that allows the firm to make a significant profit from that expense. Excessive surcharges may violate the prohibition against unreasonable fees, and may also constitute misrepresentations or misstatements about the lawyer's services—and thus may violate ethics rules such as a jurisdiction's version of ABA Model Rules 1.5, 7.1, and 8.4.

---

[103]ABA Formal Opinion 93-379 (1993).

Speed

Speed refers to how long it takes for a firm to turn work-in-progress (WIP) into revenue or dollars in the door. As a consequence of the nature of their work and their billing cycles, many law firms generally do not receive payment for their work until 60 days or more after that work was performed. For example, if a lawyer performs work on January 1, the bill for the lawyer's services likely will not be mailed to a client until mid-February. Many firms give a lawyer several days after the end of the month to get all time entered. Then the firm prints prebills, or draft bills, which the partner responsible for the matter—and sometimes every lawyer who has billing entries on the prebill—reviews for accuracy, errors in the descriptions, and the like. After such edits to the prebill are recorded in the billing entries, the bill is printed. At some firms, the bill is then forwarded to the partner for the partner to prepare a cover letter. At other firms, the billing department or bookkeeper sends the bill to the client. The prebill review process can easily take several weeks, particularly since most lawyers prefer client work over reviewing prebills.

After the bill is sent to the client, additional delays may occur. Clients often wait thirty to sixty days to pay the bill. Thus, it is not uncommon for a firm to receive payment for work done on January 1 on or after April 1. Some clients delay their payments far longer. Some large clients, for example, try to pay law firms only once or a few times per year. And often lawyers do not press to collect from slow paying clients until near the end of the firm's fiscal year, when equity partners' compensation will often be impacted by the amount of profits the firm generated, and collecting outstanding payments will improve the numbers for the lawyer and firm. Some clients also only pay their bills near year end, perhaps hoping to receive a discount if they agree to make their payment before the critical deadline.

While the firm is waiting for the client to pay for work performed several months earlier, the firm must still pay salaries, rent, and other expenses. When payment from a client is not received in a relatively prompt fashion, or the firm has just opened its doors, the firm may need to borrow money and incur finance charges for such borrowed funds until payment is received. Also, the chance for receiving 100 percent payment on bills generally decreases as the amount of time increases between the work being performed and the payment being received. This is due to the increased risk of factors that will prevent payment (such as bankruptcy or a change in financial or other relevant condition of the client), as well as human nature that people generally lose the desire to pay or justify not paying the full amount as time passes.

To increase the speed of collections, firms use a variety of policies and tools. Many firms now have fully automated and integrated time-recording and billing systems. An attorney may create a time entry on his or her computer, and the computer will automatically keep a clock running, subject to starting or stopping by the attorney. These entries are then automatically transferred to the client's prebill promptly at the end of the month. Review of the bills may also be automated, so that multiple people can review the prebill electronically, and so there are no delays as the prebills sit in envelopes or in- and out-boxes. Finally, the bill may be sent electronically to the client (some clients now require electronic billing), and payment may also be sent by the client and received by the firm electronically.

Many firms also require that time be entered within a certain period (for example, the next day, or a certain day the following week). Some firms may even punish lawyers who are delinquent in submitting their time or bills, including by reducing or withholding the lawyer's pay. Law firms also create incentives or punishments to encourage lawyers to review their prebills quickly. Each improvement in the billing process speeds the firm's receipt of payment on the bills and ordinarily improves realization.

Despite such efforts, speed in collecting bills remains a major issue for law firms. Many firms ask the partners supervising matters to get involved in collecting outstanding fees, particularly when the accounts age beyond a certain date. Firms recognize that bills not paid quickly often become unpaid bills, and that slow payment may be a sign of unhappiness with the services provided.

Health Versus Hygiene Factors

The five levers of profitability—rates, utilization, leverage, expenses, and speed—are sometimes divided into "health" factors and "hygiene" factors. Health factors, rates and leverage, tend to have a greater impact on the firm's long-term profitability. Hygiene factors, expenses and speed, have a greater impact on the firm's short-term profitability. Utilization can be either a health or hygiene factor. This depends upon the impact that the greater productivity (often higher billable hours) has on the well-being and motivation of fee-earners and the ability of the firm to develop clients, new expertise, and the like when lawyers are working very hard on work that current clients require in the near future.[104]

Management guru David Maisters complains that many firms over-manage hygiene factors and under-manage health factors. This may cause a firm to spend too much time on collecting fees and reviewing expense forms and too little time developing teams, building skills and expertise, and finding new ways to provide value to clients.[105]

---

[104] Mayson, *Making Sense of Law Firms* at 420-21.
[105] *Id.* at 421.

Client and Matter Profitability

20

In addition to firm profitability, some firms have begun to focus on how to make particular matters profitable. This requires consideration of what rates are charged—and realized—on a particular matter. It allows a firm to consider how it wants to staff a matter, or whether it wants to handle a matter at all.

It may be sensible for a lawyer or firm to take on unprofitable work, particularly if the work provides some benefit despite its lack of profits. For example, a firm may choose to accept unprofitable work because it provides at least some billable activity for otherwise dormant lawyers, training opportunities or experience, entry into a new practice group or business development opportunity, a *pro bono* or community service opportunity, or some other benefit. If every lawyer has an ample supply of billable work, however, and the firm does not perceive some non-financial benefit from the work, the firm should be willing to pass up work that will not be profitable.

In Chapters 1 and 19, we discussed an associate who would bill 2,000 hours and has overhead and compensation costs totaling $280,000. If this associate is the among the lowest-cost associates at the firm, the firm should only take work for that associate at a rate of less than $140 per hour if that work provides some non-financial benefit. After all, the firm would be losing money on work the associate performed at less than $140 per hour.

A focus on matter profitability should also cause a law firm to consider setting on particular matters. Chapter 17 introduced the following rate schedules:

	Schedule A	Schedule B	Schedule C
Senior partner	$450	$420	$280
Partner	$400	$420	$230
Senior Attorney	$350	$330	$180
Senior Associate	$300	$280	$150
Junior Associate	$250	$280	$120
Paralegal	$150	$150	$ 90

These rate structures should help guide the firm in deciding how to staff matters. The firm receives no financial benefit from having a senior partner or senior associate (as opposed to a partner or junior associate) work on Schedule B matters, for Schedule B assigns a single rate for all partners and all associates. A senior partner or senior associate may be required for a particular aspect of the representation, or the firm may choose to assign the senior partner or senior associate to the matter to derive some other benefit (for example, to give the senior associate an opportunity to try a case or to gain experience in an area in which the firm seeks to expand), but the firm should recognize it will receive no financial benefit from using such lawyers on the matter. In fact, if the senior partner or associate is paid more than a junior colleague, the firm may actually be decreasing the profitability of that matter by assigning a more expensive partner to a less lucrative engagement.

Yet Schedule B provides a higher rate for partners and junior associates than Schedule A. Thus, although the highest rates on Schedule B are lower than those on Schedule A, the firm may receive greater profits by assigning a partner or junior associate to work on a Schedule B matter instead of a Schedule A matter, even though the top rate for Schedule B work is less than the rate for Schedule A work.

Further consideration of an individual lawyer's revenue and costs may also help the firm determine how it should assign attorneys. For example, consider the junior associate who bills, earns, and costs as follows:

Hours billed per year:	2,000
Compensation and benefits:	$180,000
Overhead allocation:	$100,000

This associate must bill at least $280,000 per year to reach the break-even point ($180,000 compensation and benefits plus $100,000 overhead allocation). If the associate bills all 2,000 hours on Schedule A matters, the associate will gross $500,000 in fees and make a potential profit of $250,000 for the firm, ignoring the realization rate. If the associate instead bills all 2,000 hours on Schedule B matters, the associate will gross $560,000—a potential $310,000 profit for the firm. If the associate bills all 2,000 hours on Schedule C matters, however, the associate will gross only $240,000 for the firm—resulting in a $40,000 loss for the firm. The associate would need to bill 2,333.4 hours on Schedule C matters just to turn a profit. Alternatively, the associate could handle a mixture of work on Schedule C and on other Schedules, and thus break even or make a profit for the firm.

This discussion on individual profitability can also be expressed in graph form. Previously, Chapter 19 and this chapter referred to an associate who bills at a realized rate of $200 and re-

Billing Break-Even Point

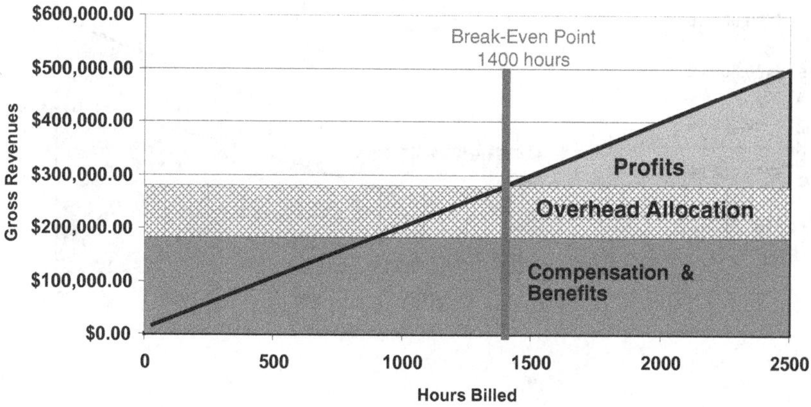

ceives $180,000 in compensation and benefits and cost $100,000 in overhead. That associate needs to work 1,400 hours before the firm breaks even.

If that same associate bills instead at a realized rate of $250 per hour, the associate would break even at only 1,120 hours. By the time the lawyer billed 1,400 hours, that lawyer would have generated $70,000 for the firm, as illustrated below.

Billing Break-Even Point

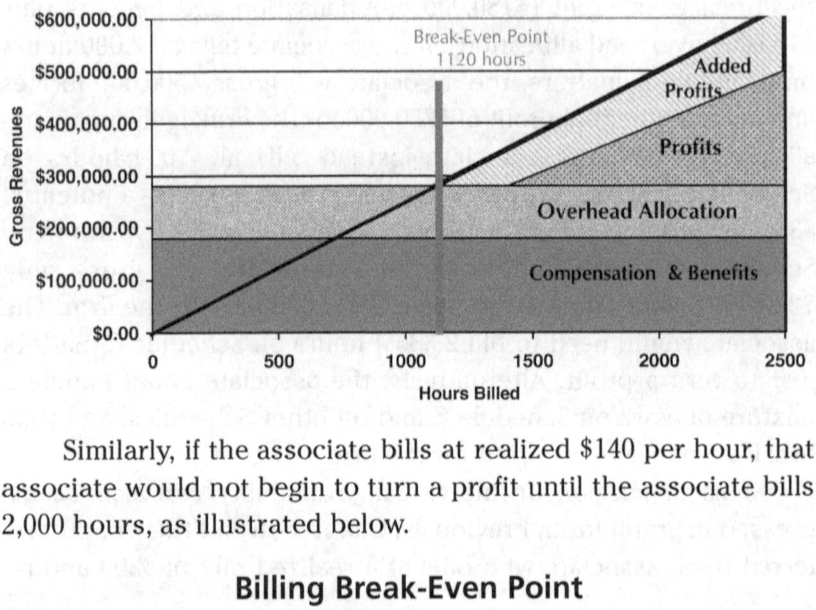

Similarly, if the associate bills at realized $140 per hour, that associate would not begin to turn a profit until the associate bills 2,000 hours, as illustrated below.

Billing Break-Even Point

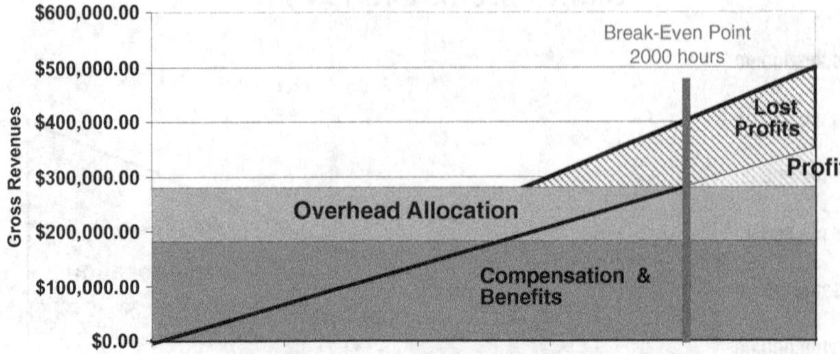

Of course, particularly at larger firms associates may have little or no ability control billing rates or collections. Often such matters are largely the partners' responsibilities.

Finally, it is important to realize that greater profits for a firm do not necessarily mean greater cost for the client. For example, suppose a client has retained a firm to work on a matter and is paying for the work pursuant to Schedule A. The firm staffs the case with a partner ($450 per hour) and associate ($250 per hour). Suppose further that the profits per hour for the partner were $150 per hour, and the profits for the associate were $125 per hour (i.e., the partner and associate cost the firm $300 and $125 per hour respectively). The matter requires work that would take the senior partner 20 hours to finish alone, or the associate 30 hours to complete and the partner 3 hours to review the associate's work.

Using these inputs, the total amounts billed to the client and profits generated are as follows:

	Scenario A	**Scenario B**	
Partner time billed	20 hours	3 hours	
Partner fees billed	$9,000	$1,350	(rate $450/hr)
Profits generated by Partner	$3,000	$ 450	
Associate time billed	0	30 hours	
Associate fees billed	0	$7,500	(rate $250/hr)
Profits generated by Associate	0	$3,750	
Total fees billed to client	$9,000	$8,850	
Potential profits generated for firm	$3,000	$4,200	

Under this scenario, the associate will take considerably more time and require some review by the partner, but using the associate will cost the client less *and* generate more profits—40 percent more, or $1,200—for the firm. Thus, both the firm and client would benefit from having the work delegated to and primarily performed by the associate. Nevertheless, particularly recently some clients have resisted allowing junior lawyers to work on their matters.

As previously noted, only some firms expressly consider client or matter profitability. Some firms or lawyers within firms do not evaluate whether a particular client or matter is profitable. Some firms consider all billable hours equivalent, even though the revenue from those hours may vary widely. At these firms, lawyers may undertake extensive matters for clients, even when the matters result in the firm losing money. For example, a firm that has some work high on the value pyramid may respond to a surge in lower-rate work by shifting lawyers from higher-rate work to lower-rate work. This may increase the lawyers' billable hours, but decrease their profitability—and possibly also decrease job satisfaction.

Problems with an Over-Focus on Profitability

21

The drive to increase profits—and concern that a failure to do so may hurt the firm by, for example, encouraging the best lawyers to leave—causes many firms to focus on profitability, often to the exclusion of other objectives. This can create a number of problems for a law firm, including:

- Profitability analyses focus on past financial performance. While reviewing consecutive analyses may provide some information regarding trends, a single profitability analysis does not reflect the current state of affairs or provide guidance for the future.
- Over-emphasizing profitability may encourage attorneys to neglect non-billable activities that may help advance other firm interests, or to cut expenses—such as training or travel—that would ultimately benefit the firm and its profitability.[106]

[106]Stephen Mayson, *Making Sense of Law Firms* 420-21 (2006).

- Over-emphasizing profitability may discourage lawyers from reducing rates to obtain a foothold in a new practice or with a new client, again actions that may provide future benefits.[107]
- Over-emphasizing profitability increases the risk that lawyers will increase billable hours either legitimately, risking burnout, or illegitimately, with potential legal and ethical consequences.
- Profitability analyses do not provide information regarding the people involved in performing the work, how they are working together, and other non-quantifiable factors. Making decisions based solely upon the numbers may result in major missteps by the firm.
- Profitability analyses do not reflect sacrifices individual lawyers may make for the good of the firm, such as changing practice groups or offices.
- Profitability analyses largely ignore business origination, and they encourage activities that may improve profits short-term but harm the firm long term, such as hoarding work.

These and other concerns often cause firms to use profitability analyses as a tool, but only a tool, for making decisions regarding management and operation of the firm.

[107] *Id.* at 421.

22 Organizing a Practice—Exercise #2

Design a firm or practice group using the following worksheet. Evaluate practice, ideal clients, and relative expenses for such a practice.

Firm Size: 2–5 6–20 21–50 51–100 100+

Practice Group Title: ______________________________

____

Practice Group Staffing: _____ Equity Partners _____ Associates

____ Other lawyers (specify) ______________________________

____ Paralegals ____ Secretaries/Assistants

Other Staff: ______________________________

Method of Billing (percentage): ______________________________

Target Market:

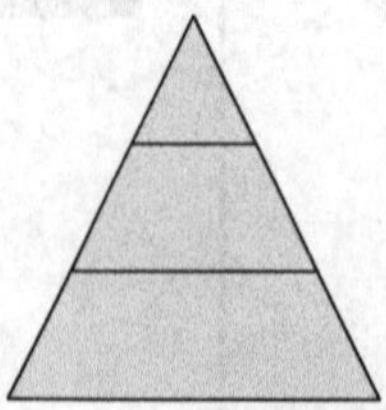

Describe ideal target clients:

____

____

____

____

____

____

Generally describe practice group:

____

____

____

____

____

Priorities for Spending:	**(Not Important)**				**(Buy the Best)**		
Office location	0	1	2	3	4	5	6
Office décor	0	1	2	3	4	5	6
Receptionist	0	1	2	3	4	5	6
Lawyers	0	1	2	3	4	5	6
Secretaries	0	1	2	3	4	5	6
Paralegals	0	1	2	3	4	5	6
Other staff (specify): ______________							
	0	1	2	3	4	5	6
Employee benefits (specify unusual): ______________							
	0	1	2	3	4	5	6
Computer technology	0	1	2	3	4	5	6
Portable technology	0	1	2	3	4	5	6
Professional association memberships	0	1	2	3	4	5	6
Charitable/community donations	0	1	2	3	4	5	6
Practice development/CLE	0	1	2	3	4	5	6

Law Firm Compensation

23

Law firms normally compensate equity partners, non-equity partners, and other lawyers at different levels. At least in profitable years, most firms generally pay equity partners more than non-equity partners, non-equity partners more than non-partners, and senior non-partners more than junior non-partners. The additional compensation often reflects higher billing rates, revenue, and value to the firm, as well as the additional risks equity partners assume.

Surveys support this trend, that higher-status and -seniority lawyers usually get paid more. According to Altman Weil, the median compensation for law firm equity partners in 2006 was $307,740. Non-equity partners received a median compensation of $200,135 and associates received a median compensation of $123,050.[108] Exceptions exist, such as when a senior partner enters a senior counsel status or a significant lawyer elects not to be a partner,[109] but these lawyers are normally quite unusual exceptions.

---

[108]James D. Cotterman, *New Survey Provides Snapshot of Law Firm Economics Across U.S.* (Aug. 2, 2007).

[109]At one Midwestern firm, one of the highest-billing lawyers was a tax lawyer who elected to be of counsel instead of a partner. He claimed he liked knowing how much money he would make, and that he did not want to assume liability for other lawyers at the firm.

Law firms also frequently use very different means to decide exactly how much lawyers at different levels should receive. This is not always the case: at some firms, all lawyers have compensation calculated using the same formula. The following section examines how compensation may be determined, how firms handle compensation reviews, and then discusses how different compensation systems may impact firm culture.

Equity Partner Compensation

Law firm equity partners ordinarily receive a portion of the firm's profits as their compensation. Because the firm's profits likely cannot be determined until the end of the firm's fiscal year (which often does but may not coincide with the calendar year), the exact amount of compensation an equity partner will receive during a year is not known until the profits are determined and distributed. Instead of being required to wait for those end-of-the-year determinations, partners are often permitted to take a "draw" or portion of their anticipated compensation on a monthly basis to cover living expenses. Often firms limit draws to a certain portion of anticipated income, or allow each partner to take only so much on a draw. If an equity partner's draw ends up more than his or her compensation, the equity partner may be required to pay back some of the money taken or to owe money due from future revenues.

In addition to not knowing until the end what the total profits will be, most law firms use a system of dividing profits that may not determine what portion of those profits each equity partner will receive until all information for the firm's fiscal year is received. Although often effectively invisible to those outside a firm, and perhaps even those outside the equity partnership, the method for determining the share of profits each equity partner will receive is among the most important differentiators between law firms and a major driver of law firm culture.

Law firms use a host of different methods to determine equity partner compensation. These include:

Fixed shares: In a fixed-share system, each equity partner receives a fixed portion of the profits. Often these are equal shares, but they do not need to be. Thus, if there are two equity partners, they may agree that each will receive 50 percent of the profits, or that one will receive a greater or larger portion of the profits (for example 60-40 or 75-25).

Fixed-share systems are very easy to administer. They often also work well when the lawyers have relatively stable practices and work habits. For example, equal division of profits often works fine among first generation equity partners who either (a) work about the same or (b) have strong personal bonds, such that one does not mind supporting the other, even for a span of several years. Fixed-share systems often break down when work habits or personal relationships change, or new equity partners feel that their compensation is suffering while they prop up the income of lawyers past their prime.

Lockstep: In a lockstep system, new partners all start at the same level, and then move up in compensation with all other members of their year or class. Sometimes compensation reaches a plateau, and then declines for a few years before a partner is expected to retire.

Lockstep compensation systems are common in leading United Kingdom firms, and are used in some American firms, notably Wachtell, Lipton, Rosen & Katz and Cravath, Swain & Moore. As of 1993 (and likely still today), Wachtell system reportedly worked as follows:

> The three founders get 125% of the average. Other seniors get 100%. Younger partners progress toward 100%. A new partner would get around 33%. These percentages are determined entirely by seniority. No one is compensated for client clout. Hours worked, client contact, and firm administration do not affect partnership shares.[110]

Other lockstep systems assign points to each class of partners. First year partners may have 10 points or shares, and a partner may receive 2 points or shares for each year of seniority after that first year of partnership until year 15. Upon reaching 40 shares in the fifteenth year, the equity partner may remain at that

---

[110]William H. Starbuck, *Keeping a Butterfly and an Elephant in a House of Cards: The Elements of Exceptional Success*, 30 J. Management Studies 885 (1993).

plateau for a period until perhaps age 60, when the equity partner loses 5 shares per year and is eased into retirement. The total profits are then divided by the total number of shares to determine a per share value. Each equity partner receives a distribution of profits equal to that per-share value multiplied by the number of shares the equity partner possesses.

In lockstep systems, sometimes partners must qualify to pass through certain gates to continue receiving pay raises. For example, using the example above, a new equity partner may begin with 10 points, and earn 2 points a year for each of the next five years. Upon reaching the five-year, 20-point mark, the equity partner may be re-evaluated before being allowed to continue progressing up the equity partner steps. In addition, some firms may have a gate at the top of the ordinary compensation system, but periodically allow a lawyer to progress beyond that gate based upon exceptional performance (particularly in business development). Thus, the example firm may general cap ownership at 40 shares, but allow truly exceptional lawyers to advance to a greater of shares.

Lockstep formulas have the advantage of rewarding longevity and loyalty to the firm, but they still lack consideration of how much a lawyer worked or what results that lawyer's efforts obtained. This can result in inequities, where more successful or hardworking partners may be subsidizing less successful or hardworking partners. Also, lockstep systems are sometimes seen as being less effective at rewarding superstars. A firm may try to mitigate such concerns by rigidly enforcing performance standards on all partners and expelling those partners who (for a single year, or more likely for several years) fail to perform at a level roughly comparable to their colleagues.

Formulaic: A formulaic system is one that uses a mathematical formula to determine what compensation a lawyer should receive.

Often, a formula is quite complex. Formulas generally focus on some aspect of client work performed (hours billed, or gross fee receipts from hours billed, for example) and some aspect of work originated (such as gross fee receipts for work originated, or billing originated), as well as contribution to the firm and its operations, reputation, and future.

In formulaic systems, some firms introduce additional elements to reflect longevity at the firm, a role in firm management, mentoring, or other activities that the firm considers commendable and chooses to reward financially. Not all such factors are weighed equally. According to an Altman Weil 2003 study discussing partner compensation systems generally:

> Personal fees collected and business origination are the two most important factors determining partner compensation in law firms. Contribution to firm management falls at the midway point in the 17 compensation factors ranked; and community involvement, professional involvement (such as writing, speaking or teaching), and seniority are the three least important compensation measures.[111]

To work as a true formula, such additional factors are often subjected to quantification and result in mathematical adjustments to the formula (*e.g.*, if the lawyer is on a firm committee, that participation is worth X dollars or X points in the compensation calculation). The result may be quite straightforward and coherent, or something that resembles a graduate mathematics course exam question and that virtually no one at the firm can comprehend. If the factors are not subject to mathematical evaluation, their inclusion would likely result in subjectivity that will make the compensation system a hybrid rather than a purely formulaic system.

Formulaic systems have the same advantage and disadvantage: they only reward what is in the formula. A formulaic approach that emphasizes one year's working receipts and fees originated may result in wide swings in compensation and ignore past performance, a history of loyalty to the firm, and how the present work may have impacted future opportunities (did it create conflicts, did the partner churn the file to generate a large fee but

---

[111]Altman Weil, Inc., *Fees Collected, Business Origination Top Determinants in Partner Compensation, Survey Reports* (Feb. 20, 2003), *available at* **http://www.altmanweil.com/index.cfm/fa/r.resource_detail/oid/4cbfa55c-cd31-4a63-81d2-58760cb2ca6c/resource/Fees_Collected_Business_Origination_Top_Determinants_in_Partner_Compensation_Survey_Reports.cfm**.

alienate a potential long-term client) as well as the risks (including professional liability) the work might create.

Formulaic systems also generally cannot account for certain types of activities that a firm wants to reward. To compensate an equity partner because that person is a team player or patient mentor, or sacrifices for the firm, or fills a present or future need at the firm, likely requires some subjective analysis.

What is worse, some equity partners will learn how to, and choose to, game the system to maximize their compensation, even if the means of doing so is hollow. For example, if a firm's formula rewards an equity partner for serving on a firm committee or mentoring, some equity partners will fight to serve on committees or be a mentor, even if they do nothing once they assume these roles. This problem may be aggravated in a system where the compensation formula changes somewhat frequently, encouraging lawyers inclined to game the system to believe they can game the system with little fear of retribution (after all, lawyers gaming the system will believe that, if the firm does not like how they are behaving, it will simply readjust its compensation system).

Subjective: In a subjective system, a group decides equity partner compensation based upon how much they believe each lawyer should receive. Sometimes that group (perhaps the whole partnership, or the compensation committee, or a particularly strong managing partner) will decide equity partner compensation with few fixed guidelines. Often firms have a list of factors considered, but the lawyers setting compensation may be free to consider or ignore factors as the lawyers believe appropriate. A subjective system may also operate as if it were a formulaic system, because the lawyers setting compensation decide some undisclosed formula is better than a more arbitrary and subjective process for assessing equity partner compensation.

Subjective systems can work very well at rewarding whatever behavior or performance decision makers consider important. The absence of objective standards, however, can result in equity partners not knowing what behavior is being encouraged and rewarded, or some may come to believe that a major factor is one's relationship with those making contribution decisions.

Subjective systems may require considerable effort to administer. At some, particularly smaller firms, the equity partners may meet once a year to fight over their compensation. Alternatively, someone must conduct surveys or request submissions and analyze the resulting information. Many such subjective systems, or systems with subjective elements, also include an interview of each equity partner by one or more members of the compensation or similar committee. All this takes considerable time and effort that otherwise could be directed to client work, business development, or other firm needs.

Hybrid: Many firms use a compensation system that contains elements of several prior systems. One Midwestern firm, for example, divides its profits up in three ways: (1) a pool from which every partner shares pro rata; (2) a pool divided based upon a formula; and (3) a pool divided based upon subjective factors. Hybrid systems generally protect against some of the problems of the prior systems, but they cannot completely vitiate those problems because the underlying elements (*e.g.*, formulaic or subjective elements that allow gaming or favoritism) remain.

In addition, a hybrid system risks being so complicated that equity partners do not know what the firm really wants, thus causing them to miss the incentives the firm may seek to create with its compensation system.

Also, purists—particularly those highly driven rainmakers who believe their billing and business origination would justify significant compensation under a more formulaic system—may become frustrated and leave for a more simplified system that fits their taste or rewards the aspects of law practice at which those people excel.

Other Traits of Equity Partner Compensation Systems

In addition to what formula is used to award equity partner compensation, compensation systems have a number of other features that can impact firm culture. One major issue is whether compensation is **open** or **closed**. In an open system, the amount that each equity partner receives, as well perhaps as how that amount was calculated, may be available to every other equity partner. This open system allows each lawyer to confirm he or she is being treated fairly, and avoids the need for blind trust. A closed system, meanwhile, removes the petty competitiveness that can sometimes mark open compensation systems. Firms vary greatly regarding how much information they share. Some firms allow all partners or all lawyers to know exactly how every other lawyer impacts the firm's bottom line. Other firms may provide no access to financial information.

Another interesting trait in compensation systems is how they credit and reward **business origination**. While many firms limit the total origination credit for a particular client or matter to 100%, some firms may allow a greater amount of credit—say 300%—to be rewarded. Thus, if three partners share equally in developing a client, all three can receive full credit for the amount of fees that client pays the firm. Such systems are designed to encourage cooperation in developing clients.

Firms also vary on what origination credit an originating lawyer can claim and for how long. Some firms allow the first lawyer that introduces a client to receive 100% credit for all that client's matters for the entire period the client is at the firm. Under such a system, a partner who brings in a small matter for a client may receive the credit when a colleague brings in significant business from that same client, perhaps wholly independent of the first lawyer's efforts. Some firms with such systems even allow a lawyer to inherit origination credits from another lawyer.

Other firms divide origination credit by matters instead of clients, or provide that a lawyer may receive origination credit for a particular client only for a few years (generally three to five years). After that time, or earlier if the lawyer who originated the client leaves the firm, the client becomes a firm client, and no one receives any origination credit for that client or that client's business.

Finally, firms differ about what **spread of equity partner compensation** they permit, the difference between the compensation of the equity partners who make the most and those that make the least. In Wachtell's system described earlier, the most junior equity partners make 33 percent of the average, more than one-fourth the

125 percent of the average the three firm founders make. Such a ratio of approximately 1:3 or 1:4, or even 1:5, is not terribly uncommon. Cleary Gottlieb Steen & Hamilton and Cravath Swain & Moore, for example, each used a 1:3 ratio as of 2007.[112] Such ratios are sometimes seen as being good to promote a cohesive firm: every equity partner sacrifices some for firm unity and peace.

Other firms may allow greater spreads. As of 2007, DLA Piper has a top spread of 10:1,[113] Reed Smith has a spread of almost 17:1, and Hogan & Hartson and Sheppard, Mullin, Richter & Hampton each have spreads of approximately 20:1.[114] Latham & Watkins has a 1:3 spread for equity partners (who receive between 300 and 900 points), but a top equity partner could make 15 times more than a non-equity partner (because Latham non-equity partners may have as few as 60 points)—or even more, because partners may also earn generous bonuses.[115] Firms recognize such vast differences in compensation may create tensions and discourage teamwork. However, some firms are more concerned about losing a major rainmaker to a firm that rewards performance more.

Finally, in some firms each equity partner is rewarded based upon their own performance, without regard for how much anyone else is making. Such firms are sometimes referred to as "eat-what-you-kill" firms. This deserves its own section.

Eat-What-You-Kill Systems Versus No-One-Starves Systems

An "eat-what-you-kill" equity partner compensation system is a system, usually formulaic, that rewards equity partners based completely or almost completely on the work they originate or the fees they collect for their own work. Such systems often empha-

---

[112]Andrew Longstreth, *Beating the Spread: Firms hunting for stars reexamine partner compensation*, American Lawyer (May 1, 2007).

[113]*Id.* Longstreth later noted that Dechert paid one equity partner $5.75 million, more than 13 times the lowest equity partner compensation. However, if the top two partners were removed, the spread would be 1:7. *Id.*

[114]*Id.*

[115]*Id.*

size the origination of client business, often looking only at one year or a small number of years.

One Midwestern firm with approximately 20 lawyers is a stark example. When client fees are received, the fees are promptly divided so that the partner who originated the work receives two-thirds of the fees. If the work for particular fees was performed by another partner, the remaining one-third of the fee goes to that partner. In any other circumstances, the remaining one-third also goes to the originating partner. The originating partner must then pay the firm a per-hour fee (which covers both compensation and overhead) for the work of any associate or paralegal who billed on the matter, and the partner must also pay a monthly fee to cover the partner's overhead. The partner keeps the rest. This resulting firm seems more a confederation of lawyers than an organized firm.

The trend, at least at larger or more sophisticated firms, is to move away from an eat-what-you-kill system toward one that rewards firm and team contributions. Such systems are sometimes called "no-one-starves" systems, and involve partners sacrificing in good years to be carried or helped in bad years. Under this present trend, while most firms still treat business origination as a major factor for compensation, a growing number of firms have stopped considering it, or reward a team for its business development instead of each individual partner for his or her development. Further, as discussed above, although at one time originations were determined on a lifetime basis (and sometimes the partner who originated the client received credit for all work from that client), the trend is toward limiting origination periods and the scope of work for which the partner originally bringing the client to the firm can claim responsibility.

Participation in Firm Management

Perhaps 20 years ago, many firms gave few allowances to lawyers who were in charge of running the firm or parts of the firm. The managing partner, practice group leaders, and the firm's general counsel or risk management partner, for example, were expected to perform and bill for client work, and to originate new business, at the level of other non-management lawyers at the firm.

In recent years, however, particularly larger firms have begun to reward lawyers more for their role in firm management. Some of the largest firms do not expect their managing partner to bill at all. Many others give partners some "billable" credit for time spent managing practice groups, addressing risk, and the like. Often, such leaders had significant practices before they assumed firm leadership and they are often among the best compensated equity partners at the firm. Firms also sometimes provide allowances for management lawyers to have a chance to rebuild their practices when they finish their period in management. For example, a firm may fix a former managing partner's compensation for three years after that lawyer stops serving as managing partner.

Compensation for Other Lawyers

Just as firms vary in how they compensate their equity partners, firms vary in how they compensate their other lawyers. Yet some generalizations are possible. Lawyers who are not equity partners ordinarily receive either (a) a salary or (b) a portion of the fees they generate, or both. They may also receive one or more bonuses based upon success of the firm, the hours they work (at firms billing by the hour), the fees they generate, the business they generate, or the success of the firm in general or on specific matters. Some firms may offer additional bonuses, for example for bringing particular matters or attorneys or other employees to the firm.

Larger firms that focus on representing corporations normally pay lawyers who are not equity partners a salary and bonus. Both vary greatly from firm to firm. The National Association of Law Placement (NALP) analyzed more than 22,000 new lawyers' starting salaries for the law school class of 2008, and found the information when graphed resulted in the following startling distribution:[116]

---

[116]NALP, *Starting Salary Distribution for Class of 2008 More Dramatic than Previous Years, available at* **http://www.nalp.org/08saldistribution**.

Distribution of Full-Time Salaries—Class of 2008

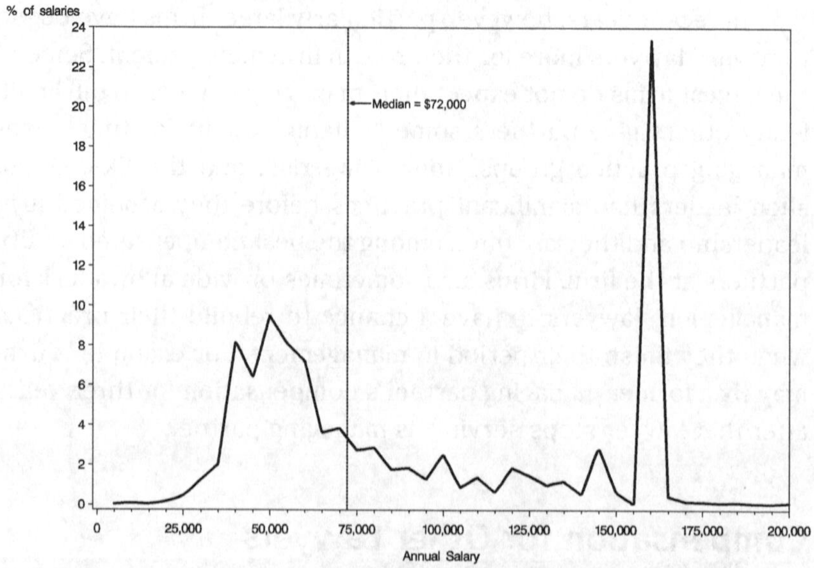

The median salary for lawyers in the class of 2008 was $72,000. The median for those starting at private firms was $130,000.[117]

This graph shows salaries for all law school graduates, including those who did not work at private firms. The salaries are clumped in two separate peaks—one between $40,000 and $65,000 (collectively 42 percent of reported salaries), and one at $160,000 (23 percent of reported salaries).[118] This second peak representing higher salaries at generally large firms has been moving to the right since the 1990s. After the economic downturn of 2008, however, many large firms have announced cuts or freezes of starting or all associate salaries. The other peak—which includes some smaller firm salaries, but is mainly lawyers not at private firms—generally did not move much since 2000, and its movement since the 2008 downturn, if any, is presently unclear.

---

[117]NALP, *Salaries at Largest Firms Peak in 2009, available at* **http://www.nalp.org/salariesjuly09**.

[118]NALP, *Starting Salary Distribution for Class of 2008 More Dramatic than Previous Years, available at* **http://www.nalp.org/08saldistribution**.

Prior to the economic downturn of 2008, the large firms that paid the highest salaries also tended to pay significant class bonuses. In 2007-08, the blog *Above the Law* (ATL) maintained detailed information on the bonuses that law firms paid associates. According to ATL's information, class bonuses—bonuses awarded to all associates of a particular class who met performance expectations—at large New York firms in 2007 ranged from 100 percent of the associate's salary (Wachtell Lipton) to no bonus. In 2008–09, the economic downturn caused many firms to cut class bonuses significantly, or to award no class bonuses at all.

Many firms also have billable hour requirements before an associate is eligible to receive a class bonus. Sometimes, the billable hour requirement is as high as 2,100 hours. Less profitable corporate firms generally do not pay class bonuses to associates.

Regardless of what happened to class bonuses in 2007–09, some large firms always did and continue to award bonuses for specific performance, such as hours in excess of minimum targets, business developed, or for bringing new attorneys or other staff to the law firm.

Bonuses for billable hours normally begin at a level of 1,800 to 2,000 hours, with bonuses being earned for each unit of 100 or 150 hours beyond the initial threshold. Sometimes these bonuses can also be quite substantial—tens of thousands of dollars—but other times they may be quite limited. Hours bonuses are often substantially less than the amount of fees generated, and often not even a significant percentage of those fees.

Firms that pay bonuses for business origination often pay some portion of the fees from clients or matters that the associate brings to the firm. The firm may impose a minimum billing rate for the work, or a threshold or ceiling for the bonuses, but business origination bonuses are often a significantly larger portion of the fees generated than bonuses for hours billed.

Other firms, including many smaller firms as well apparently as Boies, Schiller & Flexner, do not compensate associates primarily through salaries plus bonuses. Instead, associate compensation is based primarily on the revenues the associate generates. Commonly, the amount is approximately a third of what the associate generates. Sometimes these firms also pay a bonus, but this bonus normally relates to hours billed, business developed, or specific contributions to or results of the firm. It is generally not a class bonus. Alternatively, the firm may award an associate a larger percentage of fees when the lawyer also originated the matter. This compensation system is common at firms that do not bill by the hour, including plaintiff contingency fee firms.

In addition, some (generally smaller) firms—again, including many plaintiff contingency firms—offer some combination of a salary and portion of fees generated. The firm may pay a specific salary for a particular number of hours billed (often 1,200 or 1,400) or fees generated, and then share any revenues above a certain threshold. Again, additional compensation may be awarded for business development and the like.

Finally, some firms use a lockstep system for lawyers other than equity partners. In such a system, all lawyers in a particular class, such as third-year associates, receive the same salary, plus perhaps bonuses. It is also not uncommon for firms that appear to have considerable discretion regarding salary to employ a *de facto* lockstep compensation system. Such circumstances may result when a firm increases its starting salary to match competitors, but the firm's own financial situation does not fully support that salary. Firms may then offer very small annual increases in salary, particularly for associates in their first few years of practice.

This section is titled "Compensation for Other Lawyers" because firms often compensate all lawyers other than equity partners the same way. This often includes non-equity partners. Some firms, however, also treat non-equity partners as owners for tax purposes. The resulting additional self-employment tax liability—which includes payment of what ordinarily would be the employer's portion of Social Security and Medicare taxes—as well as additional expenses non-equity partners may incur by being required to pay their own health insurance and other expenses—may actually cause a non-equity partner to suffer a small drop in net income the first year or two of partnership. Moreover, if the non-equity partner is taxed as an owner, the firm may pay a portion of the non-equity partner's compensation (approximately 60 percent) in regular installments, while paying another portion (generally about 10 percent of expected annual compensation) in quarterly payments shortly before quarterly estimated tax payments are due.

Compensation and Culture

Law firm compensation is about more than money. It will often have a significant impact on firm culture. Generally, people will gravitate to conduct for which they receive rewards, including compensation. Also, lawyers tend to gravitate toward firms that share their values, or to adapt their conduct toward what is valued.

These tendencies combined with firm compensation systems often result in firm cultures that may impact junior attorneys. In an eat-what-you-kill firm, for example, lawyers are generally awarded only for the hard numbers—fees and business origination—they produce. This encourages senior lawyers to focus on billing, originating business, and collections. It does not encourage senior lawyers to focus, for example, on mentoring or teaching younger lawyers how to develop their own business. In addition, sometimes senior lawyers in eat-what-you-kill systems will hesitate to introduce junior lawyers to their clients, fearing the junior lawyer may try to take the business or credit for the business from that client.

A subjective system, meanwhile, may encourage lawyers to try to gain the favor of the people who will decide their compensation. This may result in a very political firm, or one where strong cliques develop.

As suggested above, each equity partner compensation system has advantages and disadvantages for the partners involved. Junior attorneys may also find that the compensation system for equity partners may impact life for junior lawyers at the firm.

Compensation Review Process

At many firms, at some point during the year (normally near the end of a fiscal year) each lawyer must prepare a memorandum addressing his or her performance during the year and contribution to the firm. Supervising lawyers and sometimes other lawyers or staff who have worked with the lawyer will also rate the lawyer on a number of characteristics, usually providing both numerical scores and narrative evaluations.

The evaluated lawyer may then meet with someone who will have a voice in determining the lawyer's compensation—normally a member of the compensation committee (for partners) or associate compensation committee (for associates)—and explain or defend the performance and contribution. The lawyer being evaluated may also have a chance to see and possibly respond to the evaluations prepared by other lawyers. This seems to occur, however, in only a minority of firms.

Someone, often a lawyer but sometimes a business manager or the like, will then collect information from the evaluations, the lawyer's own compensation memorandum, and interview notes, and present the lawyer to the group deciding compensation. The compensation committee will then determine appropriate compensation, often an annual raise and bonus, and disclose that information to the lawyer. At larger firms, this may be a very formal, time-consuming process. At other firms, it may be a very informal process. Of course, at firms that provide lockstep salary and bonuses, this process may be truncated because it will not impact compensation.

Performance Evaluations

In addition to the compensation review process discussed above, many law firms use a similar system in carrying out performance evaluations. These reviews may be combined with the compensation review or separated from it. The evaluation process may be timed to allow a lawyer (particularly an associate) to receive feedback on the lawyer's performance and to improve any areas pointed out as deficient. For example, a firm may carry out a performance review during the summer and the compensation review at or about year end. Some firms also encourage or require more frequent reviews, including trying to institute prompt review of junior attorneys any time a major project is completed.

Firms also vary on what information they will share with a lawyer undergoing a performance review. Some firms provide quite detailed information, allowing the lawyer under review to see who made particular comments and what they wrote. Other firms will provide the lawyer with anonymous comments, or perhaps just a summary of the reviews.

One complaint that junior lawyers often have about a firm's review processes is that they often feel somewhat ambushed by negative feedback, or they are never allowed to escape past mistakes. Although the legal profession is often adversarial, many lawyers will avoid confronting a junior lawyer about a problem at the time. Instead, the senior lawyer may mention the mistake months later at a formal review—when it is too late to correct the problem, and perhaps after the junior lawyer has repeated the mistake several times during the intervening months. Firms have made efforts to prompt senior lawyers to provide prompt feedback on such issues, but anecdotal evidence suggests that in many instances such efforts are meeting with very limited success.

24 Compensation and Culture—Exercise #3

Partners in the practice group/firm established in Exercise #2 (Chapter 22) are selecting an equity partner compensation system. Choose from the following:

Proposal #1—Equal Shares—After all overhead and expenses (including other lawyers' compensation) are paid, equity partners shall share equally in all remaining profits.

Proposal #2—Eat What You Kill—Each month, partners receive 100% of the fees they collect, unless another partner does the work. If another partner does the work, that partner receives one-third of the fee. Partners then pay a share of overhead, expenses for their own secretary, and an hourly charge for each hour of associates or paralegals' time worked on the partners' matters.

Proposal #3—50/50—Each lawyer receives up to 120 points divided so that 60 are awarded based upon quantitative performance, and 60 are awarded based upon more subjective factors as follows:

- 1-30 points for business originated (top originator receives 30 points, lowest 1, and the rest spread out proportionally to reflect their business originated);

- 1-30 points for fees generated (top generator receives 30, lowest 1, and the rest spread out proportionally to reflect their fees generated);
- 1-30 points for relationship with clients; and
- 1-30 points for contribution to the firm, all set by the compensation committee.

Profits are divided by the number of points, and then distributed on a per-point basis.

Question #1: For the equity partners, what are the advantages and disadvantages for each system?

Question #2: For the other lawyers and, in particular, associates, what are the advantages and disadvantages of each system?

25 Intake of a Client Matter

Most often, a lawyer-client relationship commences when a potential client contacts a law firm. The potential client may be responding to an advertisement, solicitation, or response to request for proposal,[119] or the potential client may know the lawyer, but still the relationship is generally initiated by the client.

When potential client contact occurs, someone at the firm must communicate with the potential client about the matter to obtain some preliminary information. At a consumer-focused firm, particularly one that advertises, this contact may be a paralegal or other intake employee.[120] For other firms, including corporate-focused firms, often a new client or legal matter comes into a firm through or because of one of the attorneys. The intake person or the attorney, who

[119]*See generally* Business Development, *supra* at Chapter 30.

[120]If the process will involve any determination as to whether the firm has interest in the case, ethics authorities may require that an attorney be involved in this process, or the evaluation may constitute the unauthorized practice of law.

is commonly referred to as the "originating attorney," will typically take down certain information about the potential client and matter. In some firms, the initial information gathered may only be the identity of the prospective client, contact information, other parties involved in the matter (adverse or not), and the general nature of the matter. This provides enough information for a basic conflict check, without causing the firm to face likely disqualification under Rule 1.18 if the firm rejects the prospective client but then seeks to represent another party to the matter. In many instances, this basic information is also virtually all the information the firm obtains before it agrees to the representation and starts working for the client.

Other firms may require much more detailed information about the potential client and engagement before a representation commences. Part of this information may be obtained—and in a more formal intake process will be obtained—prior to the running of the conflict check.[121] Then, after a conflict check is run, a lawyer or intake employee and the prospective client will communicate a second time so the firm can learn enough about the client and matter to confirm that the firm should proceed with the representation. Information obtained through these two communications will likely include the client and its principals; the client's objectives; how the client will pay and whether the client can pay; the client's past handling of the matter, including identity and dealings with any former counsel; information regarding other parties, including adverse parties, and their counsel; information regarding potential conflicts; and other information. In some firms, satisfying client intake due diligence could take a significant period of time, perhaps an hour or two.

Once adequate information is obtained and assuming no conflict or other problem prevents the representation, the firm will be ready to accept the engagement, establish the terms of the representation, and start providing legal services to the client. Some firms impose additional requirements, however, including a review by one or more other attorneys (including perhaps a designated

[121]If client confidences are obtained at the outset, this may disqualify the firm from representing anyone else in the matter. *See* ABA Model Rule 1.18.

client intake attorney) to assess whether the firm should proceed with the representation.

A matter that may create greater reputational or financial risk for a firm may receive additional, more rigorous vetting. For example, when a matter will be taken on contingency, and will involve the fronting of significant funds (e.g., for experts, depositions, and discovery), firms often engage in a rigorous review of the potential matter. Such impediments are generally lower at the plaintiff's firms, where the risk of contingency matters is accepted as part of the practice. Corporate-focused firms that only periodically dabble in contingency fee matters, however, may require an extensive legal analysis of the claims, likely defenses, and potential recovery so the firm can better assess its risks and potential rewards.

Conflict Check

Once intake information is collected, the law firm generally will conduct a conflict check. Often this check is automated: an intake person or the lawyer's assistant will run a conflict check through a firm's computerized contacts or files. Often a conflict check also includes circulation of the intake information or client intake form to the lawyers (and sometimes all staff) at the firm, so the recipients can review the information and ensure that they have checked and found no potential conflict.

Firms may involve a designated client-intake counsel early in this process, including to make sure that (a) the potential matter is one the firm is prepared (competent) to handle and interested in handling; (b) adequate information has been obtained to assess the matter and avoid potential conflicts; and (c) the firm would not cause any business or positional conflicts (*e.g.*, that a firm having an important relationship with Coke might jeopardize that relationship by representing Pepsi, or a firm that regularly represents insurance companies might jeopardize such relationships by representing a claimant against an insurance company).

After a conflict check is conducted, someone—ordinarily either the originating lawyer or the client-intake counsel or both—will review the results and determine whether there are any potential disqualifying conflicts of interest. If any such conflicts are identified, the firm ordinarily must determine whether the conflict can be waived. If so, a waiver may be sought. If a firm does not secure a waiver or the conflict is not waiveable, the firm must decline the representation.[122]

Sometimes a conflict of interest may be avoided or cured, or a waiver of a conflict obtained, by having the firm erect an ethical screen.[123] An ethical screen is a series of procedures and safeguards that prevent the taint of a conflict—usually obligations to a client or information about the client—from being spread from the screened lawyer to other lawyers at the firm. Screens also stop information and matter involvement from reaching the screened lawyer. Steps for erecting an ethical screen often include: notifying the screened lawyer of the screen's existence, ensuring the screened lawyer cannot communicate or share access or share information outside the screen, notifying affected clients about the screen, and periodically reminding the screened lawyer and others at the firm about the existence of the screen.[124] Once the screen is erected, it may permit the firm to undertake a representation that otherwise would be prohibited under the ethics rules.

Engagement Letters

After a firm agrees to accept a representation, ordinarily the firm will prepare an engagement letter or in some instances (such as when the client is plaintiff or a government entity) a retainer agreement. The engagement letter or similar document has a risk management function: it may clarify who the client is, what work the

---

[122]For more information on conflict rules and waiver of conflicts, the relevant jurisdiction's rules of professional conduct should be examined, in particular a state's version of ABA Model Rules 1.7 through 1.13.

[123]Ethical screens are defined in ABA Model Rule 1.0(k), which states "screened" denotes the isolation of a lawyer from any participation in a matter through the timely imposition of procedures within a firm that are reasonably adequate under the circumstances to protect information that the isolated lawyer is obligated to protect under these Rules or other law."

[124]For details on ethical screens and their requirements, see the various Model Rules on conflicts of interest, in particular ABA Model Rule 1.10(a)(2).

firm has agreed to do for that client, and what the firm's expectations are for the client. Engagement letters also often contain financial and other contractual terms of the relationship between the lawyer and client, for example how payments and lawyer-client communications and disputes will be handled. Finally, the engagement letter serves as one of the first communications between the lawyer and client. It helps set initial impressions and also the tone of the relationship.

If a conflict has been identified and waived, the engagement letter may contain information about the waiver of conflict (including the written confirmation the conflict was waived, which writing is generally required under ABA Model Rule 1.7(b)). Alternatively, the engagement letter may simply refer to the waiver of a conflict, and the waiver may then be memorialized in a separate waiver letter. The waiver letter will likely detail any ethical screens or other safeguards established as conditions to obtain the waiver. Also, where two clients are being represented jointly in a matter, the letter may need to address the handling of client confidences—whether or not they will be shared—in addition to the fact that the clients have decided to continue with the joint representation.[125]

Some engagement letters also contain language intended to affect the client's waiver of a future ethical conflict. The propriety and effectiveness of such waivers, which are referred to as "advance waivers of future conflicts," is discussed in ABA Model Rule 1.7 comment [22] and numerous other authorities.

---

[125]ABA Model Rule 1.7 and its comment contain requirements for a conflict waiver and written confirmation of that waiver. The primary requirements are described in the comment to Rule 1.7 cmt. [18] as follows:

> Informed consent requires that each affected client be aware of the relevant circumstances and of the material and reasonably foreseeable ways that the conflict could have adverse effects on the interests of that client. See Rule 1.0(e) (informed consent). The information required depends on the nature of the conflict and the nature of the risks involved. When representation of multiple clients in a single matter is undertaken, the information must include the implications of the common representation, including possible effects on loyalty, confidentiality and the attorney-client privilege and the advantages and risks involved. See Comments [30] and [31] (effect of common representation on confidentiality).

Retainers

Another item often addressed at the outset of a representation is a retainer. In many cases, the retainer agreement terms are included in or accompany the engagement letter. There are three major types of retainers, which the Illinois Attorney Registration and Discipline Commission described as follows:

> (1) A *classic retainer*, also referred to as a *true* or *general retainer*, is paid by a client to the lawyer in order to secure the lawyer's availability during a specified period of time or for a specified matter. This type of retainer is earned when paid and immediately becomes property of the lawyer, regardless of whether the lawyer ever actually performs any services for the client.
>
> (2) A *security retainer* is where funds paid to the lawyer are not considered present payment for future services but are intended to secure payment of fees for the future services the lawyer is expected to perform. This type of retainer remains the property of the client and, therefore, must be deposited in a trust account and kept separate from the lawyer's own property until the lawyer applies it to charges for services that are actually rendered. Any unused portion of the retainer is refunded to the client under the Illinois Rules of Professional Conduct.
>
> (3) An *advance payment retainer* consists of a present payment to the lawyer in exchange for the commitment to provide legal services in the future. Ownership of this retainer passes to the lawyer immediately upon payment.[126]

In other words, a *true retainer* is a payment that ensures the lawyer will be available as the client's lawyer for a specific period of time. For example, a municipality may pay a firm $12,000 per year to be the municipality's attorney. The attorney is then avail-

---

[126]Illinois Attorney Registration and Discipline Commission, *Dowling's New Standard for Retainers, available at* **http://www.iardc.org/DowlingOp.html** (italics added).

able to address legal matters, and will not take a matter against the municipality. The retainer may include legal services, or the client may pay additional funds for such services.

An *advance payment retainer* is effectively a type of fixed fee. The client pays the lawyer a payment—all or a significant portion of the fee—up front so that the lawyer will provide services in the future. For example, a criminal defendant may pay a lawyer $100,000 to handle a felony defense through trial.

Ownership of the funds transfers to the lawyer upon payment. But the lawyer generally must refund unearned fees if the matter terminates early, because the ethics rules in many jurisdictions prohibit non-refundable retainers and collecting an unreasonable fee. Advance payment retainers are quite common in some consumer-focused practices, particularly bankruptcy and criminal defense, because it is very difficult to collect bills sent to clients who are incarcerated or insolvent. Some states impose serious limitations on the use of advance payment retainers, primarily due to concerns that the lawyer may try unreasonably to retain client funds after termination, when those funds should be refunded to the client.

A *security retainer*, meanwhile, is not a fee payment. It is an arrangement where the client transfers money to the lawyer and the lawyer then holds the money to ensure that the client will pay for legal services received. Usually a security retainer is used in one of two ways. First, the lawyer may require the retainer to begin work, and charge fees—usually once the monthly bills are prepared—against the retainer. In other words, the lawyer works, prepares a bill, then gives the client notice that funds are being deducted from the retainer and deducts those funds. When the retainer is significantly reduced or almost extinguished, the lawyer may ask the client to provide additional funds to be held in trust. Future legal fees will then be charged against the new funds until those funds are exhausted or almost exhausted, at which time they will again be replenished. At the end of the representation, any remaining funds are refunded to the client.

Alternatively, instead of billing against the retainer, the lawyer may hold the security retainer to ensure the final bills are paid. Bills for legal services provided are sent to client, who pays those bills from other funds. At the end of the representation, as long as the client has stayed current on paying the bills, final bills are charged against the retainer and the excess is refunded to the client. A security retainer used in this fashion is quite similar to a security deposit on an apartment. The security deposit is not used to pay monthly rent, but rather to make sure that the tenant pays their bills and that the relationship ends with all financial arrangements having been addressed. If that is the case, the lawyer will refund the remaining security retainer to the client.

Such a security retainer generally must be placed in a trust account so that it is segregated from the lawyer's own property.[127] Ethics rules generally regulate the handling of retainer funds. Ordinarily, moneys that are likely to generate significant interest must be placed in an interest-bearing account where the client receives the interest. For funds not expected to earn significant interest (due to amount and duration of holding), a jurisdiction's rules may require that the funds be placed in a special Interest on Lawyers' Trust Accounts (IOLTA) account, where funds are combined and the resulting interest goes to help provide legal aid.

As a final note, the nature of the retainer must be specified clearly and in writing. Failure to do so may result in disputes with clients, ethical violations, or possible loss of funds should a client declare bankruptcy, have judgment entered against it, or the like.[128]

Prohibition on Commingling the Lawyer's and Client's Property

Note that the Illinois Supreme Court's descriptions of retainers refer several times to whose money the retainer is and where the funds must be deposited. Lawyers are normally required to keep client property, including client funds, separate from their own property and funds. The ethics rules impose very strict requirements that a lawyer must keep all clients' funds in a trust account,

---

[127] *See generally* ABA Model Rule 1.15(a).

[128] *See, e.g., Dowling v. Chicago Options Associates, Inc.*, 875 N.E.2d 1012 (Ill. 2007).

and to withdraw funds from that account only when the funds are earned by the lawyer.

Mixing lawyer and client funds (also referred to as commingling) or withdrawing client funds early—often to pay the lawyer's expenses—may result in imposition of the most severe disciplinary sanctions, including disbarment. As one legal ethics textbook explains, "Once you have a license to practice law, one of the quickest and surest ways to lose it is to put funds that belong to a client into your own account (not the client trust account) or to "borrow" funds from a client trust account that you have not yet earned."[129]

To protect client funds and ensure proper conduct by lawyers, many jurisdictions adopt special rules to govern client trust accounts. Some states limit who may serve as signatories on such accounts, and impose strict record-keeping requirements for such accounts.[130] Others require that trust funds be deposited only in certain banks, and that those banks provide notice to disciplinary authorities as soon as a trust account is overdrawn.[131] Such efforts may result in swift investigation and possible discipline for lawyers, including newer lawyers, who have trust account issues. Bar counsel in several states report receiving notice that a trust account is overdrawn quickly—sometimes less than a month—after a lawyer has learned he or she had passed the bar and opened his or her practice. As these anecdotes suggest, trust fund rules should be studied and followed carefully by any lawyer who receives money from clients.

---

[129]Lisa G. Lerman & Philip G. Schrag, *Ethical Problems in the Practice of Law* 469 (2005).

[130]*See generally* Indiana Supreme Court Rule 23 § 29.

[131]The American Bar Association even has prepared Model Rules on Trust Account Overdraft Notification, as well as similar rules for financial record-keeping and handling funds in such accounts. *See* **http://www.abanet.org/cpr/clientpro/contents.html**.

Time-Billing Entries

26

For lawyers who must keep billing entries (either because they use time-based billing or because they may need to prove time spent on a project; for example, to recover a court-approved recovery of fees), the creation of billing entries will likely involve considerable time and effort. Bills are generally client communications, so billing entries must communicate what the client is paying for—what the lawyer has done and how it has moved the client's matter forward. Billing entries must also be accurate: a lawyer who misstates billable hours may face disciplinary action.[132]

The relative importance of billing entries have caused many firms or subgroups in firms (such as a partner or practice group) to adopt conventions for how billing entries should be worded. Where such conventions have been adopted, a junior lawyer should follow those conventions. The following is offered as guidance when a firm or practice group does not provide its own guidance.

[132]Inflated bills may violate ethics rules that prohibit lawyer fraud and misstatements and require reasonable lawyer fees, for example Model Rules 1.5, 7.1, and 8.4.

The basic format for time entries is often as follows:

- [Verb] [object] with/for [prep object] regarding [prep object]

Use either title and last name or generic title for persons. For example:

- "Conference with Dr. Smith regarding deposition of plaintiff's cardiology expert" (where client will recognize Dr. Smith) or
- "Conference with cardiology expert regarding deposition of plaintiff's cardiology expert" (where client will not recognize the doctor).

Other examples include:

- "Review memorandum regarding possible removal of case to federal court." (Recognizing that client may not know what "removal" is.)
- "Research Maine law regarding liability for a dog bite."
- "Telephone conference with court clerk and counsel for Acme Corporation regarding setting hearing for motion to compel written discovery responses from Acme Corporation."

Some recommend adding even greater detail, that the lawyer state not only what was done but why. An example might be:

- "Research Maine law regarding liability for a dog bite to include in summary judgment motion that may result in judgment for plaintiff in case."

Such entries help the client understand the value of the work done, but most lawyers do not use such billing entries. Also, some lawyers or clients use far more (or less) detail than is suggested here.

When preparing billing entries, lawyers often try to use similar language to describe an activity. For example:

- "Draft" "draft/revise" instead of *write*, *type*, etc.
- "Correspondence" for any type of letter
- "Memorandum" for any internal firm communication

- "Review"—not *look at*
- "Email [recipient]" instead of "Draft email to . . . "
- "Telephone conference with" "instead of *talk on telephone with*
- "Review and organize file"
- "Travel to . . . for"

Use "same" instead of repeating information. Thus, an entry may state:

- "Travel to Los Angeles for negotiation of sales contract; review file for same en route."

Finally, sometimes lawyers will record on a bill tasks they perform for a client but do not intend to bill to the client. The activity can be recorded with an indication that 0.0 hours were billed to it, or the time could be billed at a rate of $0 per hour. For example, if you do work for Client A while traveling for the Client B, the billing entry for Client B may read:

- "Travel to Los Angeles for negotiation of sales contract (2.4 hours not billed)."

The 2.4 hour, could then be billed to Client A, and subtracted from travel time otherwise billed to Client B. Such entries notify the client of what was done for them, even when it is not billed to them. This is also a good remedy to the frequent complaint clients have that it costs them money every time they speak to their lawyer.

Billing time is a huge hassle. Most lawyers that move from time-based billing to other systems—in particular, to in-house roles—normally revel with the freedom they feel after they no longer need to capture all billable time.

To avoid making matters worse, a lawyer should try to accurately capture time at or near the time work was done. This allows the lawyer to be fair with himself or herself, his or her firm, and also the client. (A senior colleague once told me jokingly that his firm should hire a clerk to follow him around and record his time. The lawyer mused the additional time captured would more than pay the clerk's wages.) A lawyer will also avoid spending hours trying to reconstruct their time if they maintain some sort of time records contemporaneous with the work they are doing. This may be simple notes, or it may be detailed time records. Many firms use special time-keeping software that simplifies the process, for example by allowing a lawyer to quickly select a client/matter number from a drop-down list, use shorthand the computer recognizes to create a meaningful and readable description, and then turn off and on a clock to keep track of how much time is actually spent on a client matter.

Finally, a lawyer often can only bill 60-80 percent of the time spent at the office. Certainly on some days—when working on a major project, meeting with clients, or in deposition or trial—the lawyer may be able to bill a much greater portion of the day. However, calls with family, friendly discussions with colleagues, lunch, trips to the restroom, and quick checks of favorite non-legal Web sites should not be billed to clients. These types of activities often take far more time than a lawyer may anticipate.

27 Managing Client Work

Law firms continue to evolve how they perform client work. Some work is susceptible to uniform treatment, and such work may effectively be automated. Other legal work requires careful individual attention of senior lawyers. Most legal work lies somewhere between those extremes.

Rather than become lost in the labyrinth of such distinctions, this chapter addresses several processes for how legal work is handled. In particular, this section addresses client and matter teams.

A *client team* or *matter team* is often an ad-hoc gathering of lawyers and nonlawyer assistants who work on a file. A "team" may consist of a single lawyer working alone, or a small or even large group of lawyers and paralegals. Normally, a more senior or specialized lawyer will direct the efforts and supervise the work of more junior lawyers. The junior lawyers may each handle a separate part of the representation, such that they are all operating effectively as co-equals (even when significant differences in seniority exist). For example, a matter team may appear as follows:

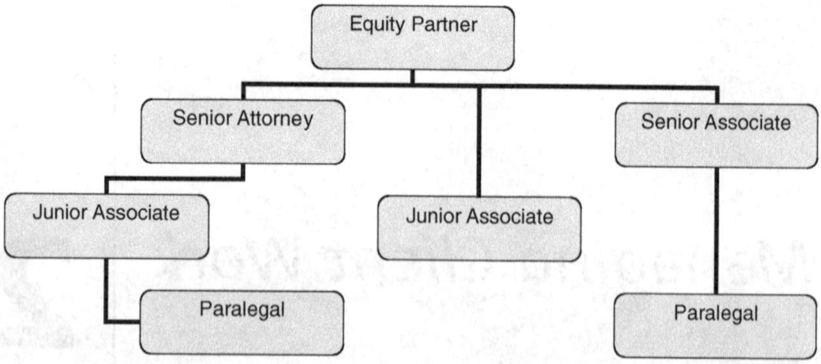

The equity partner directly supervises three lawyers, one of whom supervises a smaller team of a junior associate and paralegal, one of whom works alone, and one of whom supervises a paralegal. For a different or smaller matter, the equity partner may choose to work with only one other lawyer or even just a paralegal.

As law firms have become more sophisticated, they have also begun to convert a team, normally a *client team*, into a relatively permanent group of people. A client team may include lawyers of varying seniority and with varying types of expertise who work on various aspects of matters. For example, a law firm that has a major banking client may establish a client team that includes banking lawyers but also employment, litigation, and real estate lawyers. Each lawyer is quite familiar with the bank, its employees, and its way of doing business, and brings a different expertise to address that client's legal needs. The firm can then also expend resources making sure that the firm knows of changes at the client and is adequately meeting a client's needs.

Such client teams are nothing new: firms such as New York's Milbank Tweed Hadley & McCloy had such a team for a major banking client decades ago. Regardless of whether a permanent client team exists, many firms will establish a *relationship partner* who has responsibility for monitoring a firm's interactions with a client and ensuring the client is pleased with the firm's work. The relationship partner may be the originating partner, or it may be another lawyer whom has the firm has designated to fill this role (which is a very important role for a major client). The relationship partner may also be part of a firm's efforts to provide succession planning, so that a client will continue to use a firm after an originating partner resigns or retires. In such instances, a law firm may consult with a client and make sure the client approves of a chosen relationship partner.

Some firms also expand the client team model to form *industry teams*. Again, lawyers in an industry team may have varying expertise, but all focus on providing legal services to a particular industry. Thus, instead of serving a single banking client, a permanent client team may be expanded to include more banking, employment, litigation, real estate, and other lawyers, all of whom commonly provide legal services to banks.

Such client or industry teams are common at many types of law firms. A plaintiffs firm, for example, may have a group of lawyers who handle a particular type of claim. Often such teams are formed based upon a particular partner's practice, instead of some conscious decision by the firm.

Pro Bono 28

In addition to work for paying clients (or at least clients expected to pay), lawyers are encouraged or sometimes required to perform some type of *pro bono* (literally "for the good," short for *pro bono publico* "for the public good") legal work.

What Is Pro Bono—at Least to Firms and Bars?

As the term is normally used, including in ABA Model Rule 6.1 and by most law firms, *pro bono* generally includes five categories of activities:

1. *Legal assistance to those of limited means.* This may include, for example, helping indigent tenants in disputes with their landlords, or helping persons of limited means with their taxes or family law matters.
2. *Legal assistance to organizations that aid those of limited means.* This includes providing legal services to organizations that help those of limited means, such as groups that provide housing, education, and related services.

3. *Direct legal assistance for other non-profits.* Pro bono also generally includes legal work performed for other non-profit or charitable organizations, such as civic, cultural, educational or religious groups.
4. *Efforts to improve the legal system.* Normally this work includes either efforts within the legal system—such as serving on bar committees focused on improving the legal system—or providing educational or similar outreach to students or other groups outside the legal system.
5. *Financial contributions to law-related groups.* This may include financial contributions to legal aid groups, and also contributions to groups whose mission is to improve the legal system or legal profession. (Normally contributions to judicial or other candidates are not treated as *pro bono* contributions.)

Not everyone agrees that all five categories should count equally as *pro bono*. Some believe, for example, that a lawyer who serves on a charity board with other corporate and civic leaders should not receive the same credit as a lawyer who deals directly with and represents those of limited means. Others believe that only time, and not money, should be considered when evaluating *pro bono* contributions. Still others criticize firms that take credit for *pro bono* activities, but then also seek to recover their fees as a prevailing party in such a matter.

The five categories also do not encompass all good works a lawyer may perform. The major category not reflected is the donations of time, money, energy, and other resources that lawyers make to groups that are not law-related. For example, bar associations or firms may count—under a version of ABA Model Rule 6.1, a reporting requirement or option, or the like—hours spent doing legal work for a housing assistance organization, but not time spent at that same organization actually building a house.

Participation in Pro Bono

Firms engage in *pro bono* for a broad range of reasons. Sometimes these reasons also influence how *pro bono* is encouraged, or what projects a firm undertakes. Many firms or firm leaders see *pro bono* as a personal, moral, or professional obligation, as public or other service that "good" lawyers or people do. Many firms also recognize that *pro bono* provides training and opportunities, particularly for younger lawyers to assume major responsibility in matters. In addition, *pro bono* activities may provide marketing or branding opportunities for a firm, including helping firms rank high on certain legal media or similar reports, and helping the firms attract and retain certain lawyers and clients.

Firms use numerous methods for encouraging *pro bono*. Some firms require that all lawyers at the firm provide a certain amount of *pro bono*. For example, in August 2006, Dechert began requiring all firm lawyers to perform 25 hours of *pro bono* each year. Failure to comply is apparently treated as a factor when determining lawyer compensation.[133] Weil Gotshall expects each lawyer to perform 50 hours of *pro bono*. Recently it required lawyers to specify *pro bono* projects as part of their annual reviews, and to explain if their *pro bono* hours are low.[134] Many other firms merely encourage, or strongly encourage, firm lawyers to perform *pro bono*.

Whatever method is used, some firms report significant *pro bono* participation. In 2007, for example, about 14 of the 200 highest grossing corporate firms reported lawyers averaged more than 100 *pro bono* hours per year, and more than 10 such firms reported that 75 percent of their attorneys performed at least 20 hours of *pro bono* in 2007.[135] Dechert's mandate may have paid dividends: it led the way with 98.1 percent of its lawyers reporting more than 20 hours of *pro bono*. Jenner & Block, meanwhile, reported the highest average per lawyer, 174.8 hours per lawyer.[136]

Firms also often count time spent on *pro bono* work toward lawyers' billable hour requirements. Sometimes the amount of time that may be counted is limited (often to 100 or 200 hours), or hours

---

[133]Nate Raymond, *Pro Bono Report 2008: A Silver Lining to Economic Downturn?*, The American Lawyer (July 14, 2008).

[134]*Id.*

[135]*Ranking the Firms: 2007 Pro Bono*, The American Lawyer (July 14, 2008), *available at* **http://www.law.com/jsp/article.jsp?id=1202422684066**.

[136]*Id.*

above a certain level may count toward billable hours only with management or other authorization.

In reality, firms view *pro bono* work very differently. Some firms place a real interest and emphasis on *pro bono*, rewarding those who make legitimate efforts. Others may provide lip service to *pro bono* work, but otherwise ignore time spent on *pro bono* or similar activities. Some such firms focus only on revenue-generating activities, and compensate attorneys based only on the business and revenues they generate.

Selection of Pro Bono Projects

Just as firms vary in how they view *pro bono*, firms vary in how they select and coordinate *pro bono*. Some firms have a designated lawyer or nonlawyer coordinate all firm *pro bono* projects, including selecting the projects where lawyers' attention should be directed. Other firms have a coordinator or committee that is involved only in particular matters, such as assessing whether to grant billable hour credit for a larger, more time consuming project. Still others allow each lawyer to select his or her own project, with little or no firm coordination or involvement.

Other Firm Civic and Charitable Work

Finally, in addition to *pro bono* projects, many firms require or expect lawyers and non-lawyer staff to undertake civic or charitable projects. This may range from group participation in fundraisers, toy collections, or home building to encouraging participation in certain fundraisers. Such activities are often seen, as noted before, as being good for the firm reputation as well as for the community and camaraderie they encourage.

While most of these activities are commendable, one problematic activity that reoccurs quite frequently at law firms deserves particular mention. Lawyers and other staff are often encouraged to donate funds to particular political causes or candidates. Sometimes the person asked to give such a donation is promised reimbursement from the firm. Often such arrangements violate state or federal campaign donation laws.[137] Lawyers should therefore be very careful before requesting or agreeing to such an arrangement.

[137]*See, e.g.*, Federal Election Commission, *Citizen's Guide* (Updated Jan. 2007), *available at* **http://www.fec.gov/pages/brochures/citizens.shtml** (discussing prohibitions against donations in the name of another, such as a corporation paying bonuses or otherwise reimbursing employee donors).

Business Development 29

Background and Ethical Framework

One area of law firm operations that has undergone major change since the 1960s is law firm business development. Prior to the United States Supreme Court's 1977 decision *Bates v. State Bar of Arizona,*[138] state ethics rules barred virtually any type of lawyer advertising.

In 1977, after some favorable precedent regarding other commercial speech, Arizona lawyers John Bates and Van O'Steen challenged the premise that the First and Fourteenth Amendments allowed states to ban lawyer advertising. They ran the advertisement on the next page.

Bates and O'Steen then proceeded to litigate whether Arizona could prohibit such advertising. Ultimately, the Supreme Court held that "advertising by attorneys may not be subjected to blanket suppression." False and misleading advertisements may be restricted. But advertising that is not false or misleading may be subjected only to "reasonable restrictions

[138]433 U.S. 350 (1977).

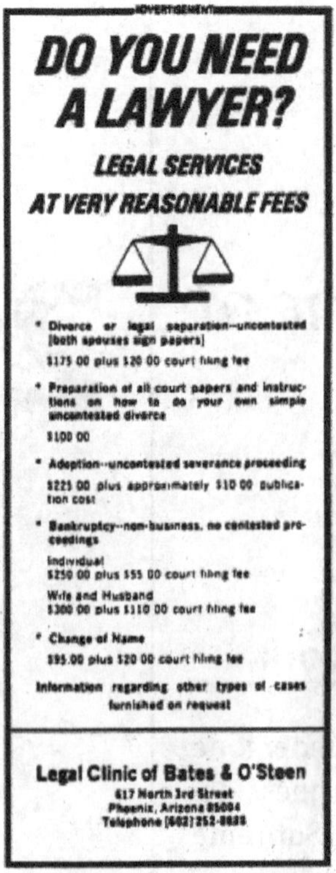

on the time, place, and manner of the advertising."

After *Bates*, a series of Supreme Court decisions provided guidance on what restraints are constitutional. *Ohralik v. Ohio State Bar Association*[139] held that generally states may prohibit in-person solicitation of clients for pecuniary gain. *Shapero v. Kentucky Bar Association*[140] held that states may regulate but not prohibit direct-mail solicitation of potential clients known to need certain legal services. Other decisions provided additional guidance on other advertising and solicitation issues.

Responding to these and other court decisions addressing the constitutional limitations on regulation of lawyer advertising, the ABA has prepared model Rules 7.1 to 7.4 to address limits for lawyer advertising. Basically, these rules provide:

Rule 7.1—False and misleading communications—including private communications and advertising—about a lawyer or the lawyer's services are prohibited.

Rule 7.2—Lawyers may advertise, including in print, radio, television, and other public advertisements, but they must comply with certain additional rules. Also, lawyers may pay regular advertising costs, but they may not pay nonlawyers to refer cases.

Rule 7.3—Lawyers may not engage in in-person and real-time (such as telephone) solicitation of nonlawyer clients except when the lawyer is related to or has a pre-existing personal or professional relationship with the prospec-

[139]436 U.S. 442 (1978).

[140]486 U.S. 466 (1988).

tive client. Also, when sending a potential client known to need particular legal services a solicitation letter, the lawyer must satisfy certain additional requirements.

Rule 7.4—Lawyers generally cannot claim to be an expert or specialist in a particular area of the law, unless their state bar recognizes and the lawyers achieve such certifications, or certain disclaimers are made.

In addition to these restrictions, a number of states have adopted more onerous restrictions including rules that prohibit the use of client testimonials, limit the images and sounds that can be used, and the like.

Before a lawyer seeks to develop his or her business, he should familiarize himself with the rules of the relevant jurisdiction. Further, because Rules 7.1 and 7.4 apply to virtually all communications about the lawyer, including private statements, all lawyers—including those not advertising—should take care to comply with these rules whenever communicating about themselves, their qualifications, or their practice.

Now, we turn our attention to where and how law firms develop business. Such efforts are divided into two categories: (1) business development efforts to prospective clients, and (2) efforts to retain and expand services provided to existing clients.

30 Developing Business from New Clients

Law firms' efforts to develop business from new clients vary greatly. Some firms, particularly consumer-focused litigation firms, recognize that most of their clients will have only one or a limited number of cases on which the firm could work. These firms may devote considerable time, energy, and resources—in rare instances one-third or more of the firm's gross revenues—to pursuing new clients.

Other firms, particularly certain specialized corporate-focused firms, may expect to continue performing legal work for an existing client or group of clients for the foreseeable future, and may effectively neglect developing business from new clients. Some firms, for example, receive almost all their work from a single insurance company or a small group of insurance companies. These firms, particularly a so-called "captive firm" that is "captured by" an insurance company and exclusively or almost exclusively represents the insureds of that company, may see little need to pursue new clients. Or a firm may have a particular type of practice—for example, representing utilities, a particular type of government entity or contractor, or other unique, limited groups of client companies—where few opportunities to develop new clients exist.

Most law firms operate somewhere between these two extremes. Such firms devote some portion of their resources—often a relatively limited amount, frequently less than 5 percent of gross revenues—to developing new business. The flow of new business is often crucial to the survival of the firm: even firms that have relatively stable work and clients find that over time changes in regulation, the market for services, or at clients may necessitate that lawyers and firms locate new sources of business. Many firms compensate lawyers for developing new business, sometimes to a greater degree than they would compensate lawyers for developing the same work from existing firm clients.

Law firms also vary greatly in what means they use to develop new business. In fact, it seems that law firms use almost every conceivable means for developing new business. Certain firms—usually at least one in every major market—have well-developed television and radio advertisements that attract the attention and business of at least some segment of potential clients, often victims of medical malpractice or automobile or work-place accidents. Others purchase lists of persons involved in particular legal matters, for example, recent arrest or foreclosure reports, and mail solicitations to those potential clients. Still other firms rely on more traditional means of business development, including participation or leadership in bar and civic organizations, encouraging referrals from business leaders and lawyers, or engaging in *pro bono* or other activities that may build the firm's reputation. Law firms have used specially-branded sports and office equipment, alcohol bottles, condoms, cars, and t-shirts launched from boats to seek clients.

This Chapter provides a brief overview of some of the many means lawyers and law firms use to develop work from new clients. It does not and could not cover all means that firms use. However, it does attempt to provide an introduction and summary of common means lawyers use to promote their firms to new clients, as well as some of the ethical dangers such business development techniques may involve.

The materials are divided into two major sections, advertising and non-advertising promotional methods. This division is to provide a framework, but it should not be seen as exclusive. Often a non-advertising promotion will include providing a prospective client with printed or other recorded messages (and thus advertising materials) about the firm. For example, at a business lunch or in-person meeting, a lawyer might give a prospective client printed material or a DVD about the firm or a particular practice group or substantive area of law. Also, often advertisements are intended only to supplement or draw attention to the firm's non-advertising promotional activities, for example a newspaper advertisement that announces a law firm-sponsored seminar or event.

Finally, virtually all means of seeking clients are governed by state ethics rules. As noted in Chapter 29, many ethics rules govern specific types of client solicitations, such as ABA Model Rule 7.2 governing advertising and ABA Model Rule 7.3 governing in-person and directed, mailed solicitations. This text attempts to at least reference such rules during the discussion of the relevant method for soliciting clients. Lawyers should be aware that other rules—including state-specific rules—may govern virtually any form of solicitation. In addition to these rules, three particular rules provide important limits on the content of client solicitations and payment arrangements for developing new clients. First, ABA Model Rule 7.1 prohibits a lawyer from making false or misleading statements about the lawyer or the lawyer's services. This includes advertising communications.[141] Second, although lawyers may pay advertising costs, lawyers may not pay nonlawyers for providing referrals.[142] Third, although Model Rule 1.5(e) generally allows a lawyer to share fees with another lawyer not at the same firm in certain circumstances, Model Rule 5.4 generally prohibits a lawyer from sharing fees with a nonlawyer.[143]

[141] ABA Model Rule 7.1 cmt [1].
[142] ABA Model Rule 7.2(b).
[143] ABA Model Rule 5.4(a).

Advertising Promotions.

ABA Model Rule 7.2(a) provides that a law firm may "advertise services through written, recorded or electronic communication, including public media," as long as such advertisements comply with other portions of Rule 7.2 and, as appropriate, other ethics rules. Model Rule 7.2 as adopted has been held to govern virtually all types of recorded communications, including television, radio, and written materials ranging from firm brochures to telephone directory listings to roadside billboards to business cards, as well as similar communications provided on the Internet such as webpages, webcasts, banner advertisements, blawgs (legal blogs), directory listings, social networking site posts or virtual world posts, and the like. Specific types of lawyer advertising include:

Radio and Television Advertising. Law firm television and radio advertising spending and content vary, with certain consumer-focused firms leading the way in spending and in the creativity of their message delivery. According to the Nielsen Monitor-Plus, the legal services industry spent $575 million television on advertising in 2007. The top 10 spenders were all consumer-focused personal injury firms, the now-named Sokolove Law, LLC leading the way with approximately $25 million spent on advertising.[144] Many of the most notable lawyer advertisements are from this group of primarily personal-injury firms that have elected to use television advertising to attract potential clients. They will often purchase 30 or 60 second commercials, and run professionally prepared and produced advertisements including on local and national broadcasts.

Yet television and radio advertising is not exclusively for consumer-focused firms. In 2001, the now defunct Brobeck ran what was heralded as the first television advertising campaign by a corporate-focused firm. This campaign cost approximately $5 to $6 million that year.[145] Today it is quite common to see or hear announcements that corporate-focused firms are sponsoring broad-

[144]Maria Aspen, *Getting Law Firms to Like Commercials*, New York Times (June 19, 2007).

[145]Brenda Sandburg, *Brobeck Cuts Paralegal Supervisors,* The Recorder (March 15, 2002).

casts, in particular of financial and sports programming. Most of these announcements, however, are "tombstone" announcements—primarily text on a single-color or otherwise relatively plain screen, and thus similar to a tombstone—instead of the more creative, often attention-grabbing advertisements that consumer-focused firms such as personal injury firms may run. Corporate firms also sponsor numerous civic, charitable, and other activities, and ensure their name and other pertinent information appears during or after such broadcasts.

Directory Listings. Lawyers have also long used directory listings to seek new clients. For decades, lawyers have used telephone directories—including full page advertisements, as well as advertisements on the spines and front and back covers—to promote their services. Lawyers have also used lawyer-specific directories such as *Martindale-Hubbell* to list their background, contact information, and credentials.

The increased availability and convenience of the Internet have increased the use of similar Internet directories. Lawyers now often include practice and contact information on community directories, bar association directories, and directories for other groups such as local chambers of commerce, industry groups, and the like.

Two specific types of lawyer directories have become more common—and in the lawyer regulatory community more controversial. The first is "premier lawyer" listings. Some of these, notably *Best Lawyers in America* and the lawyer-rating system in *Martindale-Hubbell*, have existed for many years. But in recent years other premier lawyer lists have become far more common. These lists may identify lawyers rated as the premier lawyer in a region or the premier lawyers in a particular practice area.

Such premier lawyer lists are controversial for three reasons. First, they are sometimes thought to contravene long-standing, and in some jurisdictions still active, advertising regulations that prohibit or discourage lawyers from using advertising content that compares the quality or other aspects of the advertising lawyer's services to those of other lawyers unless the comparison can be factually verified. (These regulations would permit, for example, a firm to say it is the "oldest" or "largest"—because those characteristics could be factually verified—but not "best" since which firm was the "best" could not be factually verified.) Second, many critics believe a lawyer's presence on a list indicates a lawyer's popularity or willingness to pay to be on the list or for other advertising from the preparer of the list, rather than the lawyer's ability to handle legal matters. Third, while many jurisdictions permit a lawyer to advertise the lawyers' inclusion on the "premier" lawyer list, sometimes lawyers exaggerate the significance of their inclusion on the list and claim they are "premier lawyers" instead of merely stating they are "listed on" or "included in" a particular premier lawyer list. In light of these concerns, lawyers asked to participate in a premier list may want to ensure that the list and related activities comply with the applicable ethics rules, in particular their jurisdiction's versions of ABA Model Rules 7.1 and 7.4.

The second type of directory that has become more prevalent and controversial in recent years is online lawyer match or referral services. These services normally allow a potential client to conduct a search and identify lawyers who engage in certain types of practices within a certain area, for example bankruptcy lawyers in a particular city. The listed lawyers normally pay to be included in the match service. The prospective client searches for, locates, and contacts listed lawyers. The prospective client and a particular contacted lawyer can then determine whether the lawyer will represent the client. An alternate system involves having the potential client provide a summary of his or her legal matter that either all or selected member lawyers can then review and, if they are interested, contact the potential client.

Such online match services raise three major ethical issues. First, match services raise concerns about how the service is paid. Lawyers may pay reasonable fees for advertising services, but lawyers may not pay a nonlawyer to refer cases to a lawyer, nor may they share fees with a nonlawyer.[146] Lawyers participating in online directories must be very careful, therefore, how much and on what basis the match service is paid. Second, sometimes the

---

[146]*See* ABA Model Rules 5.4(a) (limit on sharing fees with nonlawyers) and 7.2(b) (limit on payment of referral fees to nonlawyers).

match service may make representations regarding the qualifications of listed lawyers that violate ethics rules. For example, a match service may overstate what lawyers must do to participate in the match service, or exaggerate the credentials or expertise of those lawyers included in the match service. Third, lawyer match services sometimes have nonlawyers screen cases and determine which listed lawyers should receive notice of potential client inquiries. Such screening by nonlawyers without lawyer participation may constitute the unauthorized practice of law.[147]

Printed Materials. Perhaps the most common law firm marketing materials are printed materials. An advertising message may be printed on large billboards, on paper as brochures or magazine or newspaper advertisements, business cards, or posted on the Internet on firm or third-party websites. The content, appearance, and sophistication of such materials vary widely. Almost every firm has some form of firm resume or brochure that describes the firm, including its history, operations, and practice areas. Firms also generally have, either in that firm brochure or separately, descriptions of individual practice groups and lawyer resumes. Often such printed materials are prepared by firm lawyers or marketing personnel, sometimes working in a format or pursuant to a template the firm has established.

Many firms supplement these printed materials with a host of other printed advertising materials that vary as to content and purpose. Some firms use print advertisements, often with pictures and other messages, that are posted on billboards; placed in legal, business, industry, or general newspapers and magazines; or prepared as separate fliers. Firms may also prepare written newsletters, case alerts, and the like, although the ease of electronic newsletters and the cost of printing and mailing paper documents are often making such materials obsolete.

---

[147]The ethical issues that arise from participation in online matching services are discussed in numerous advisory opinions, including Arizona Ethics Opinion 99-06, Massachusetts Advisory Opinion 06-06, Maine Ethics Opinion 174 (2000), Rhode Island S. C. Ethics Advisory Panel Opinion 2005-01, South Carolina Ethics Advisory Opinions 01-3, Texas State Bar Ethics Opinions 561 and 573 (2006), and Washington Ethics Opinion 2106 (2006).

Virtually every law firm uses some form of printed marketing materials, often with little controversy. Of course, such materials must comply with the ethics rules, in particular the relevant state's version of ABA Model Rules 7.1, 7.2, and 7.4. Two types of written communications deserve particular attention: (1) solicitations directed to persons known to need particular services, which are sometimes called *Shapero* letters, and (2) responses to requests for proposals ("RFPs") and requests for information ("RFIs").

Directed Solicitations. Some law firms, normally those that seek to represent consumers, use mailings directed to particular persons known to face particular legal issues. When these mailings are sent to people with identified legal issues or concerns—such as persons recently arrested for particular crimes or those facing foreclosure—they are sometimes referred to as *Shapero* letters after *Shapero v. Kentucky Bar Association* cited earlier.[148] Such *Shapero* letters generally must comply with strict, state-specific restrictions normally contained in a state's version of ABA Model Rule 7.3. These restrictions often include (a) not disclosing the nature of the legal problem where it may be viewed by others; (b) conspicuously marking the mailing as advertising material, often in red on the envelope and first page; and (c) telling the prospective client how the lawyer learned the prospective client faces the specific legal problem. For example, a letter to someone facing prosecution for driving while intoxicated should not mention DWIs on the envelope, and should indicate in the letter's text that the lawyer learned the potential client's name by reviewing arrest records or purchasing a list of arrestees from a third party.

Firms and lawyers responsible for *Shapero* letters should be very careful about what is said in such letters and to whom those letters are sent. Also, firms considering sending such communications in electronic form (*e.g.*, as emails) should make sure the messages comply with state and federal regulations governing the sending and receipt of unsolicited emails as well as state ethics rules.

Requests for Proposals and Requests for Information. Requests for Proposals ("RFPs") and Requests for Information ("RFIs") are

---

[148]*See* Background and Ethical Framework, *supra* at Chapter 29.

written requests from prospective clients. Law firms may not consider their responses to such requests as lawyer advertisements, but in reality such responses are a specific type of directed written solicitation.

A Request for Proposals ("RFP") is a document, often several pages, that invites law firms—or, in other settings, other types of vendors and service providers—interested in providing legal services to an entity (often a public entity or perhaps a private company) to submit a detailed proposal for the provision of such services. The RFP establishes criteria that must be satisfied, ranging from types of lawyers who will serve on the team and relevant legal experience to minority participation, insurance and indemnification requirements, and references. The RFP may also include other detailed questions that must be answered, including information about fees and budgets. Generally, an RFP requires that a complete submission—often a large document, perhaps 30 or more pages in length—must be submitted by a particular deadline. Submissions that are not timely or complete are often rejected on these bases.

A Request for Information ("RFI") is similar to a request for proposals, but generally is not intended to result in a contract for provision of legal services. A potential client, usually a corporate or public entity, requests information from potential legal service providers regarding their capacity to provide certain legal services. Often the RFI requests information on a limited area of practice, and seeks to receive that information in a certain format.

The requesting entity can then use the RFI responses to compare providers and assess their capabilities. For example, the University of Texas uses an RFI process to identify potential legal providers for educational institutions within the University of Texas system. The UT general counsel's office places firms that respond to the RFI on a referral list. These firms are not guaranteed work, but may be contacted by a member institution that has a particular type of legal service. Generally, such firms are instructed not to expect $25,000 or more per year based upon their inclusion on the referral list.[149]

---

[149] *See* Outside Counsel: Law Firm Selection, University of Texas System website, available at **http://www.utsystem.edu/OGC/outsidecounsel.htm** (visited May 2009).

Review processes for RFPs and RFIs vary considerably, but usually involve between two and four steps. First, the requesting entity prepares the request and solicits responses, often by publishing the request in a government publication and in newspapers and on the Internet. Second, the requesting entity reviews responses submitted. After this review, the entity may select the winner, or it may arrange a third step, an in-person meeting with top candidate firms akin to the "dog-and-pony show" discussed below, before selecting a winner.

Once a winner is selected, the final step often differs for an RFP versus an RFI. In the case of the RFP, the final step normally involves the requesting entity entering an agreement with the selected firm so the firm will provide legal services consistent with the proposal. The contract may detail a particular project, or provide the law firm will handle a type of legal work on particular terms, often for a period of one or more years. In the case of the RFI, meanwhile, the winner or winners may simply be placed on a list of potential providers that the requesting entity may use in the future to select a law firm to provide particular services.

Law firms respond to RFPs and RFIs in a variety of fashions. Some law firms eschew RFP and RFI processes, believing that preparation of an RFP or RFI is too much of a burden for too little benefit. These firms may also believe entities request proposals or information not to locate new providers, but only to gain leverage to seek discounts from current service providers. Other firms regularly respond to RFP/RFI requests. In fact, in certain legal fields such as government finance work, much of the legal work is distributed through RFP/RFI processes.

Firms also vary widely in how they prepare RFP/RFI responses. Some firms put relatively little effort into responses. They may have marketing professionals or nonlawyer staff compile pre-existing resources, even if those resources do not perfectly match the request. Other firms expend considerable resources in preparing a response. They may involve senior lawyers and other highly qualified staff in the response preparation. They may also use special software to select appropriate materials, and modify those materials to tailor the materials to the needs and interests of the requesting entity.

A newer lawyer who becomes drawn into preparing a firm's RFP/RFI responses should realize that preparing such responses is time consuming and often thankless. Preparation of the submission may take dozens of hours, or longer. Often, the firm will not receive any work from a response. Alternatively, the firm may receive some of the work, but the lawyer who prepares the response often will not receive credit for generating the new business. Instead, the senior lawyer who received the RFP/RFI or the senior lawyer designated as the anticipated leader of the team will receive the credit for new business generated through an RFP/RFI response.

If the newer lawyer works at a firm that rewards such activities, however, participation in preparation of an RFP/RFI may be a rewarding activity. Involvement in the RFP/RFI process may allow the newer lawyer to work with leading lawyers in the practice. The newer lawyer may also have an opportunity to meet with an important client or potential client as part of the "dog and pony show." The newer lawyer may also receive credit for helping develop new work, either individually or through recognition for that lawyer's office or practice group.

Internet Advertising. Obviously the Internet has provided numerous channels for all types of businesses to pursue potential customers through multiple channels, and many businesses are taking advantage of such opportunities. Many law firms are likewise devoting considerable time, energy, and resources developing an Internet presence. Often this consists of a firm website, which normally provides a firm history or summary; credentials and contact information for the lawyers (and, on occasion, other staff); a list or description of practice areas; news updates about the firm or areas in which it practices; and contact information for the firm. Many firms have added other, more creative content to their websites. This may include blawgs (blogs on law-related subjects), webcasts, and other information about the firm, fields in which it practices, or recent developments in substantive law.

Law firms are also taking advantage of third-party sites. Some firms encourage their lawyers to participate in social networks like Facebook or LinkedIn, to locate or maintain contact with friends and acquaintances, answer questions, and post materials about current developments. Law firms have created complicated firm sites in virtual worlds such as Second Life, and posted lengthy videos (including firm commercials, client interviews, and substantive presentations) on third-party sites such as YouTube. In addition, some law firms are purchasing advertising or paying to receive sponsored links when certain search terms are used on Internet search engines. Firms regularly report great success in developing new clients or new business from existing clients through such efforts.

Most of these activities are akin to and regulated like previously mentioned advertising. For example, a webcast will often be regulated similar to a radio or television advertisement, and the content of a website will be regulated in a manner similar to the regulation for a firm's printed materials. Yet the Internet creates a number of particular risks, three of which deserve attention here.

First, the Internet and other electronic communications such as email have a global reach. Lawyers can reach potential clients in any jurisdiction, and provide those potential clients with legal guidance regarding any type of legal matter, including one wholly in the client's home state. Such conduct may constitute the unauthorized practice of law, however, and thus violate the version of ABA Model Rule 5.5 as well perhaps as criminal unauthorized practice statutes or other laws in the client's jurisdiction. Some state regulators even consider offering to provide legal services in a jurisdiction as the practice of law in that jurisdiction.

Second, lawyers need to recognize that providing specific, tailored legal advice likely creates a lawyer-client relationship. Thus, if a lawyer answers questions on a social network or other Internet site, that lawyer may be deemed to have created an attorney-client relationship with the questioner, despite the fact that the questioner has not agreed to pay a fee and other formalities of a relationship are likely missing. Also, providing advice without running a conflict check or taking other precautions usually employed when evaluating a new client or matter may expose the firm to unforeseen risks.

Third, electronic information tends to travel far and last forever. Thus, law firms and lawyers must be careful to ensure they do not disclose client confidences or make statements harmful to the firm or its clients, particularly on the Internet. To mitigate such risks, some firms ask lawyers who are blogging or otherwise placing information on the Internet to undertake certain precautions before posting online communications. These precautions may include avoiding certain topics and running a conflict check before posting communications about particular cases or partners.

Non-Advertising Promotions.

In addition to printed or recorded advertising communications, law firms often engage in a variety of live and in-person activities that seek to promote the firm or its lawyers and their expertise and to develop new business. These programs include large firm-sponsored events, either on a substantive area of law or perhaps related to or in support of a community activity. Some firms spend considerable time, efforts, and resources preparing, promoting, hosting, and presenting on substantive topics at meetings either for local lawyers or business people or even a national audience of persons interested in a particular topic. These meetings may be one-time, annual, or repeating events, and may target a particular group or promote a particular practice group, or seek to promote a firm's diverse practices to numerous audiences.

Law firms also sponsor local events, perhaps a local fair or community, art, or sports event, and then invite persons to attend the event as guests of the firm. Firms also sponsor community or service projects, such as canned food drives or building projects for the homeless, and then encourage clients, friends of the firm, and others to contribute to the success of such activities.

Law firms organize and fund more limited events. Lawyers may invite potential clients to share a drink or meal, hoping to get to know the potential client better and increase the likelihood the potential client will retain the law firm. These meetings may be rather random (sometimes referred to as "random acts of lunch"), or they may be part of an organized and targeted effort of the firm or its lawyers. Law firms also organize live programs, including in-person, telephone, and web-based programs, hoping to attract potential clients, reaffirm relationships with existing clients, and establishing the firm or its lawyers as experts in a particular area of law.

Law firms not only organize events, but they seek to promote themselves, their lawyers, and their practices through events that others sponsor. Some lawyers or firms work hard to position themselves as leaders of civic, bar, and other groups, so they can meet important people or further the interests of the firm, perhaps by having their firm name appear in program materials or their lawyers speak or moderate at group events. These events, like events that firms sponsor, vary greatly and include everything from substantive programs on legal issues to programs or events that have nothing to do with the law or substantive legal issues.

Dog and Pony Shows. Law firms often use the term "dog and pony show" to refer to formalized meetings with potential clients. This term does not refer to a casual marketing lunch or similar activity. Rather, it refers to a meeting usually between several representatives of the law firm and several representatives of the potential client. Sometimes, the dog and pony show is part of the RFP/RFI process. In such circumstances, several firms may make presentations, sometimes in quick succession. Other times, it is a separate meeting where a law firm has somehow gained the concentrated attention of a potential client to consider using the firm's lawyers.

Many law firms effectively script their dog and pony show presentations. They will often have a set team—often three to five attorneys of diverse practice, ethnic, and other backgrounds and features—who are prepared to present a firm's positive face to a potential client. Often these lawyers will use a tailored computer presentation and printed materials to display the firm and its capabilities to the potential client.

Unsolicited In-Person Solicitations of Strangers. One type of activity that legal ethics rules severely restrict is in-person or real-time (usually telephone) solicitation of potential clients by lawyers. Under ABA Model Rule 7.3 and the comparable rule in most jurisdictions, a lawyer may contact a prospective client directly to solicit business only if the prospective client is a lawyer or the lawyer and person contacted have a familial, close personal or prior professional relationship. These restrictions generally cause law firms to avoid cold calls or similar efforts to solicit new legal business. Yet firms also recognize that personal contact is often the best way for lawyers and law firms to obtain business from existing or former clients, or from non-clients. This realization is a primary reason that firms place such emphasis on substantive programs, community involvement, and other activities that allow lawyers to initiate relationships with potential clients that will ultimately allow the lawyer to solicit business from the client under ABA Model Rule 7.3.

Runners. Another type of law firm solicitation that ethics rules severely limit is the use of nonlawyers, sometimes called "runners," to solicit new business. Runners typically are persons paid to identify and retain prospective clients. The use of runners is normally prohibited for two reasons. First, the use of runners as agents to solicit new clients in person violates ABA Model Rules 7.3 (the general prohibition against in-person solicitation) and 8.4(a) (which prohibits a lawyer from violating the ethics rules including through the acts of another). Second, runners often receive compensation based upon the work they help originate, which may violate limits on paying for referrals (contained in ABA Model Rule 7.2) and sharing legal fees with nonlawyers (contained in ABA Model Rule 5.4).

Self-Marketing

In addition to firm-driven marketing, most lawyers undertake their own personal marketing efforts. Such efforts normally develop either the lawyer's expertise and experience or the lawyer's interpersonal relationships, or some combination of the two. A lawyer may join a civic group, for example, to meet people in the community. This would help develop interpersonal relationships. Or a lawyer may write an article for an industry publication. This would help establish an area of expertise. Or the lawyer may attend a lunch and present on substantive legal issues to an industry group on a subject. This would develop both interpersonal relationships and expertise/experience.

In part, the target market for a lawyer's services should help determine where a lawyer devotes his or her time for marketing. A lawyer who wants to develop a very high-expertise practice will need to develop that expertise. Often, this may be done while working for clients under a senior lawyer who also practices in the area. However, the junior lawyer may also need to devote non-billable time to developing personal expertise, expanding the niche beyond where the senior lawyer is established, or building a practice or industry group not already at or thriving at the firm.

There are no sure-fire methods for developing business. There is, however, a lot of common wisdom on business development, including the following seven points:

First, a newer lawyer should make sure that he or she does good-quality, timely work at or under budget. A firm's senior lawyers offer major sources of opportunity for training and for work. A newer lawyer should work to make sure a senior lawyer is happy and proud to include that newer lawyer on a client team, to work with that newer lawyer, and to have that newer lawyer meet and communicate with clients and potential clients. Current clients are also major sources of additional business, either more of their work or as references or referral sources for other clients work. If a junior lawyer consistently does legal work well, in a timely fashion, and at a reasonable cost, this should help ensure that the lawyer will satisfy the most basic needs a client has. Failure to satisfy these needs, however, can significantly reduce the likelihood that client will send the newer lawyer more work or recommend the newer lawyer to others.

Second, it often helps if a newer lawyer narrows his or her focus for business development. Lawyers, particularly newer lawyers, tend to believe that they need to be prepared to provide any legal services that any client may need. This is probably true in very lightly populated areas. In cities and more densely populated areas, however, studies generally show that a lawyer will benefit from narrowing the scope of legal work he or she targets for development. The lawyer can then build referral relationships with lawyers who handle other types of cases. This helps the lawyer build a referral network, and also decreases incidence of "dabbling," an activity that often results in unhappy clients and potential malpractice and other risks.

Also, although a lawyer should take care to avoid overspecialization, a newer lawyer will likely benefit from choosing one or a few practices or industries on which to focus your business development efforts. Lawyers who do focus nevertheless receive referrals on other matters, and can then assess whether they want to handle the matter or refer the matter to others either at their firm or at other firms. Listing a long and varied group of practices is normally seen as an indication that the lawyer does not know any area of practice well. This does not instill confidence in prospective clients.

Third, a newer lawyer should treat people like they may refer business, but not necessarily try to get business from them. When I began practice as a litigator at a larger corporate-focused firm, I believed every person I met was a potential client. Later I realized that, for the firm to really benefit from a matter, it had to be a case or group of cases where the client could pay $20,000 or more in fees. In reality, most people would never have a case that crosses this threshold. This realization allowed me to focus my business development efforts on those people likely to have work, and to relax a bit when such prospects were not around.

Of course, this is not to say that a lawyer should mistreat anyone, even a person that does not appear likely to become a client. Often legal work comes from unexpected sources. A partner received a very significant referral from a potential lateral candidate, who moved to another firm and then (because of a conflict) could not represent the client at that new firm. Also, often associates or law firm staff may leave a firm to go in-house. The experience these people had while at the firm, with lawyers at their own firm as well as at other firms, often decides what firms will receive their employer's legal business.

Thus, a newer lawyer should try to treat people well—the interpersonal relationship side of business. But a newer lawyer does not need to spend every working hour trying to convince every person he or she meets to hire the firm. Sometimes a lawyer can and should just relax, as long as "relaxing" does not involve irresponsible, unethical, or rude behavior.

Fourth, newer lawyers are encouraged to develop a plan. Many resources and guides exist for developing personal marketing plans. Lawyers are normally well served if they develop a very practical business development plan and stick with it.

For such a plan, it is often suggested that lawyers adopt personal, concrete actions that the lawyer creating the plan can control. The plan may specify, for example, that the lawyer will have lunch with two people a month from a chosen industry. This approach is generally considered better than planning, for example, to develop ten new clients, without setting out the basic steps the lawyer can control and use to reach the goal. Often it is better for a lawyer to specify what the lawyer will do, write, or speak, instead of listing outcomes to be accomplished.

Fifth, a lawyer should commit to engaging in business development on a regular basis. Some lawyers only market when they do not have client work to do. The problem is that inevitably a slow time will come. If a lawyer neglects business development while busy, this absence of business development will likely result in the lawyer having little to do for pay when the lawyer comes off a busy period.

Many business development experts instead advise that a lawyer should spend an hour a day or a few hours a week, every week, on business development. This may be writing an article or preparing a speech. Or it may be having lunch with or speaking on the telephone with an industry or client contact. Whatever the case, such consistent business development efforts will help build the expertise and relationships necessary to develop business. It will also help protect against troughs in a lawyer's workload.

Sixth, communicate, communicate, communicate. A lawyer should keep clients informed and keep in touch with referral sources, prospective clients, and past clients. Lawyers often send useful information to such people so the recipient knows the lawyer is thinking of them, and so the potential referral source thinks and thinks well of the lawyer. This helps the lawyer come to mind when the potential client or someone they know needs a lawyer.

Seventh, and perhaps most difficult, a lawyer seeking to develop a practice needs to be patient. Sometimes experts say that it takes at least three, five, or seven years of sustained effort before a lawyer should expect to have substantial business from business development efforts. Even meeting this timeline may require some hard work and associated good fortune. A lot of lawyers who have been practicing a decade or more, and who have been trying to develop business during that period, still barely have enough work to keep themselves busy.

The Elevator Speech

Lawyers are often encouraged to develop an "elevator speech" as part of their self-marketing, branding, and business development efforts. An "elevator speech" is a very short, specific description of what a lawyer does. It is suitable for quick delivery in response to the question, "What do you do?" Business development advisors recommend that it be positive and indicate the type of work the lawyer does and for whom the lawyer does it, and that it should invite further conversation about the lawyer and his or her practice.

Generally, elevator speeches are about 30 words in length, although some advisors suggest longer or shorter messages. All the words in an elevator speech should be easy to say and remember. If a lawyer states that he or she "facilitate international asset-based securitization arrangements," this is less appealing than saying, "I help global companies obtain financing for large new plants and projects," and then expanding on this point.

Some experts advise lawyers not to use the words "lawyer" or "attorney" in their elevator speech, because such words turn people off. They also advise lawyers to emphasize traits such as that they are "problem solvers." In some instances, this may be good advice. In other circumstances, however, such terms are necessary to tell the listener what the lawyer does. If a trial attorney tells people, "I help people solve disputes with commercial partners," this may not really tell the listener what the lawyer does.

How Much Do Firms Invest In Developing New Business?

Business development now is generally among the largest expense for law firms, often after employee compensation and rent. At some firms, particularly consumer-focused high-volume practices, advertising expenses may be the single largest non-personnel expense of the firm.

Even corporate-focused firms that largely avoid radio, television, and similar advertising, and who may view the words "legal marketing" with disdain, often invest significant resources in business development efforts. The 650-lawyer firm Duane Morris LLP, for example, employed approximately 40 marketing professionals prior to the 2008 economic downturn. At least one large law firm has more than 70 marketing professionals. And sometimes chief marketing officers make $500,000 or more.

That said, many firms devote only a percentage or two of gross revenues, or less, on business development. Often junior lawyers should expect to invest their own resources—particularly their time, energy and enthusiasm—in their business development efforts.

What Works for Business Development?

What works for lawyer marketing? As previously noted, there are no clear "sure-fire" ways to develop clients. Certain activities, however, are consistently identified as being good ways to develop business. A law firm consulting group, the Remsen Group, surveyed corporate-focused law firms and found the law firms identified the following business development activities were successful for developing business:

61%	Visiting clients
9%	Firm-sponsored seminars
12%	Organizational Involvement
3%	Speeches
0%	By-lined Articles
2%	Web site
3%	Newsletter
10%	Other

Consumer-focused firms would likely provide a very different list, but such data is not as readily available. While most surveys indicate that television and telephone directory advertisements still generate significant revenues for law firms, many question their effectiveness—particularly of telephone directories—as Internet usage increases.

31 Retaining Work from Existing Clients

Law firms—particularly corporate-focused firms—may also spend great energy trying to teach young lawyers to help the firm maintain existing business from current clients. Firms recognize that current work is necessary to finance the future of the firm, that most new work comes through existing clients, and that marketing to and developing additional work from existing clients will cost far less than trying to cultivate new clients. (Some estimates indicate developing a new client may cost ten times more than developing additional work from an existing client.)

How are existing clients maintained or developed? First, the client must be happy with the work they are receiving. This involves making sure that quality services are provided in a timely fashion and for a reasonable price. It also requires the lawyers to communicate well with the client, including (a) keeping the client reasonably informed (in a sensible, coherent manner) about the status of the matter; (b) demonstrating an understanding of the client, the client's business, and how the matter fits into the business; and (c) communicating legal expertise—or at least competence. Lawyers have notorious habits of ignoring telephone messages and emails and otherwise not communicating with clients. Firms generally encourage all lawyers, but particularly younger lawyers, to avoid such tendencies.

Second, the client must know what other services the law firm can provide. Often this involves trying to communicate with the client or arranging social outings or gatherings (lunch, firm events, and the like) where a client may meet other lawyers at the firm and learn the type of work those lawyers do. Law firms will also forward cases, firm publications, and announcements to the law firm's clients in the hopes that the client will retain the law firm for some other purpose. Such activities are often referred to as "cross selling."

Third, the client must retain the law firm for the additional matter. Sometimes, this may be as simple as letting the client know the firm is ready to provide the necessary services, and encouraging the client to engage the firm. In other instances, firms are more aggressive, sometimes even offering a free or discounted service in the hopes of proving their mettle and obtaining future work in a new area.

Client Relationship Management

32

To facilitate developing new business and maintaining existing business, some firms have invested in and are using client relationship management (CRM) software programs. Such programs allow particularly corporate-focused law firms to organize information (also called "relationship intelligence") that they have or receive about existing and potential clients.

Basically, CRM programs organize and improve searchability of information about clients or prospective clients, their operations, and their people. Using CRM, a lawyer could determine who else at a firm knows someone at a prospective client or keep track of communications they have had with that prospective client. Some firms have also developed the ability to determine, for example, which events a prospective client attends or which article links are used by particular recipients of practice group email newsletters. This information allows the firm to better understand their relationship with a client or prospective client, and to assess how to further that relationship.

33 Lending Clients Money

Under the current ABA Model Rules, a client may be relieved of the obligation to reimburse a lawyer for litigation expenses if a matter is not successful. A lawyer may not, however, advance other funds—for medical bills or living expenses, for example—to a client. The advance of such expenses is generally prohibited under a state's version of Rule 1.8(e). In some jurisdictions, Rule 1.8(e) has also prevented a lawyer from personally guaranteeing a client's financial obligations.

34 Sample Business Development Checklist for Associates

The following is a checklist prepared by Kelly A. Blazek, former Director of Client Relations at Hahn, Loeser and Parks in Cleveland, to help associates at that corporate-focused firm. It is also available at **http://www.lawmarketing.com/pages/articles.asp?Action=Article&ArticleCategoryID=9&ArticleID=62**, and is used with permission of Ms. Blazek. As you review this list, notice that many suggested activities do not require a significant investment of resources or significant expense. Suggestions of such methods for building prospective client relationships and expertise are quite common for young lawyers.

First-Year Associates

- Create a mailing list and keep it updated. Who goes on it? Your law school classmates, your fraternity/sorority contacts, college friends, etc.

- Take at least one person out to lunch or to an event every quarter. Write a follow-up note on note cards.
- Join a bar association.
- Send out holiday cards to your mailing list.
- Sign up to have the firm's annual report sent to your mailing list. Participate in firm client functions.
- Encourage senior attorneys to introduce you to clients you don't know, or go ahead and introduce yourself and thank them for being our guest.
- Send out "saw this item and thought it would be of interest" mailings.

Second-Year Associates

- Get involved in your community through committee or volunteer work. People you serve on a committee with should be added to your mailing list.
- Keep adding to that mailing list with the names of accountants, bankers, and clients you're working with.
- Volunteer for a bar association committee.
- Write an article for your area or practice group.
- Increase those lunches and events with your peers.

Third-Year, Fourth-Year, Fifth-Year Associates

- Offer to host a committee meeting here at the firm for a volunteer group you're in.
- More lunches, sports, or cultural events. You should be entertaining a peer once a month.
- Join the professional trade associations or organizations in which your clients are members. The firm will help you research local chapters and events.
- Write articles on topics of interest to professionals in your industry—the marketing department will get them in the firm newsletter as well as place them in trade publications and general business magazines.
- Present a speech to professionals in your industry (if you wrote an article, well, hey, that's sort of a speech ready to go, isn't it? Shake the paper a little, and voila!)

- Continue involvement in bar associations—committee work, Young Lawyers activities, editorial work on the publications, volunteering to organize an educational event.
- Increase your direct contact with clients.
- Offer to be the editor of your section or area's newsletter.
- Help senior attorneys and partners at firm seminars. Offer to present a topic.

Sixth-, Seventh-, Eighth-Year Associates

- You should be setting annual business goals. Work with your Area/Group Development Chair to fill in the appropriate number in the following statement: "I want to be responsible for bringing in $_ thousands in originating collections this year."
- Take on leadership positions in bar and trade association groups.
- Have two lunches or events with prospects, clients, and referrers per month.
- Keep up community involvement by running for board positions in organizations you've joined. Make certain the firm is financially supporting at least one fundraiser, bike-a-thon, golf outing, or young friends benefit a year that you're directly involved in.

Client Service Checklist

- Be punctual at meetings. Your client's time is incredibly valuable.
- Make a client feel as though they are the only piece of business you work on! Don't discuss how busy your other clients are keeping you. Remove your other clients' files from your desk when you meet, and never tell a client you can't get back to them/handle their question because "I'm doing work for other clients and it's a rush."
- Return phone calls promptly. This is one of the largest complaints clients have of their lawyers in general. If you are so tied up that you can't return the call, have your secretary call and say "Sue will be freed up at 4:30, you are the

first call she's going to return, and is there anything I can do to help in the meantime?" Setting expectations is a big part of communicating with a client—if they know when they'll hear from you, they can live with a four-hour delay—which is far preferable to feeling as though they've been ignored.

- Don't strand a client in the reception area if they are coming to meet with you and you are tied up. Have your secretary or a colleague greet them, offer them coffee, take them to a conference room, offer them the phone for calls, etc.
- Use language in general business correspondence that your client understands; they're the one that is driving the relationship, not you. Make yourself understood, and you'll be seen as "my business partner that talks my language" instead of "I'm never sure what my lawyer is talking about."
- Note, remember and USE names of your client's team—their receptionist, their secretary, their managers. Support staffers are the gatekeepers to your client, and fostering a good relationship with them can be just as important as one with the client. Who else will sneak your call in when the client is "too busy to answer the phone?"
- Take a tour of your client's facility, offices, factory, or stores. Meet employees, ask questions, and become more familiar with the issues their industry faces.
- When great news like a settlement check or a signed contract that took weeks to negotiate arrives at the firm, personally drive it to your client and deliver it with a smile and a handshake.
- Is a special event coming up for your client? A new headquarters move? An anniversary? Were they named to a distinguished list or did they win a prestigious industry award? Mention and celebrate their success with them.
- Remember, if you can't provide client service like this, your competition at another firm is glad to!

35 Marketing a Practice—Exercise #4

This exercise provides an opportunity to consider how the practice created in Exercise #2 (Chapter 22) should be marketed. Complete the following worksheet, trying to align marketing methods to the firm's target clients.

Practice Group/Firm Focus: ______________________________

Target Market:

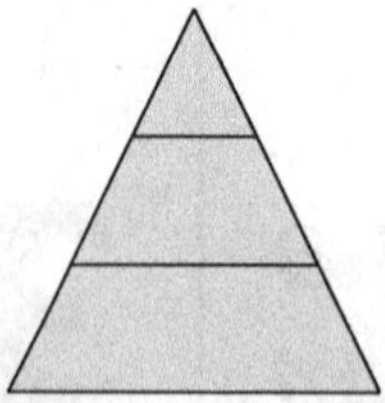

Describe ideal target clients:

____

____

____

____

____

____

What will you do to market your practice?

____

____

____

____

____

____

Use of Promotions—Explain Use:

Television: Y or N	Radio: Y or N	Newspaper: Y or N
Magazines: Y or N	Internet: Y or N	Phone Directory: Y or N
Seminars: Y or N	Social Events: Y or N	Directed Mail: Y or N

What is your elevator speech?

____

____

____

____

____

____

36 Firm Culture and Demands on Time

Different firms place different expectations on how lawyers will use their time. Such demands can create a great deal of tension, but also offer a host of different avenues for resolution.

Arrival and Departure Expectations

The practice of law, technology, and billable hours create a fair amount of flexibility in a lawyer's schedule. A lawyer can perform work and bill hours during the middle of the night, and this work or hours count the same as work performed during middle of the day, particularly now that email, electronic court filing, and other technology allow for the filing or delivery of work also at almost any hour. Thus, a lawyer may come into work late and then work late, often with no perceived adverse impact on the firm or the client. For many firms, the only real issues are that the work is completed and, when relevant, the hours are billed, not when.

This resulting "flexibility" may have two downsides. First, for lawyers with significant billable hour requirements or goals, the temptation may be to wrack up billable hours and never take time off. Thus, vacations or trips away from the office become opportunities to bill in a different location, instead of chances to get away from work. This problem can be severe for younger attorneys, as they feel the weight of needing to meet more senior lawyer's expectations. However, it can often continue as seniority rises, because the lawyer will likely feel the same pressure from client expectations.

In such a pressure cooker, work or billable hour expectations may become more significant than vacation days for young attorneys. Some firms tell lawyers that they have three or four weeks of vacation a year, but then impose stringent billable hour requirements on the lawyer so that most lawyers take far less time off. Also, firms may have other policies on billing that make the burden of the billable hours even greater.

For example, a law firm may have agreements with its client that prohibit lawyers from billing for travel time when no substantive work is performed, and such policy may only aggravate the burden a young lawyer feels. The young lawyer may leave home at 6 a.m., drive four hours, and after a short delay participate in a five-hour deposition or client meeting that begins at 10:30 a.m. Then the lawyer drives home, arriving home at perhaps 8 p.m. or so. If the lawyer cannot bill the travel time, and the lawyer is expected to bill 2,000 hours per year, the lawyer will still need to bill about three hours to stay on track—even though the lawyer has already worked 14 hours on that day (because only the 5-hour meeting or deposition was billable). Also, some firms enter arrangements with their clients where a significant portion of a lawyer's time cannot be billed. For example, a firm may agree that only one lawyer can bill for reviewing a pleading, or that no one can bill for time meeting with other lawyers at the firm, even on matters when multiple lawyers need to review documents, meet, and coordinate their efforts.

Over time, the pressure that results from the expectation to bill, and also the impediments to billing, can have serious detriment on the mental and physical health of young lawyers. Also, a temptation will arise—sometimes reinforced by actions of more senior lawyers at a firm—to misrepresent hours, to bill clients for time that either ethics rules or client agreements do not allow the lawyer to bill (perhaps by fudging work descriptions). Such duplicity will also create considerable stress, and may expose the firm and its lawyers to disciplinary and other liability—including possible criminal charges.

Second, the apparent flexibility lawyers have may collide with a firm's expectations about how a lawyer should work. In several instances, more senior lawyers have expressed frustration that younger lawyers do not appear to take their work seriously because the junior lawyers arrive later or leave earlier than more senior lawyers. For example, if everyone else arrives for work by 9 or 9:30 a.m. at a law firm, an associate may be seen as less punctual or hard working if that associate arrives typically at 10:30 a.m.—even if that associate works later than other attorneys, or leaves at the same time as everyone else but then works from home for several hours. Arriving late periodically may be deemed acceptable, but always arriving later may be perceived as a sign a lawyer is not committed to a firm or its clients. Also, if senior lawyers typically work part of the weekend, they may expect hard-working and diligent junior lawyers to work that part of the weekend as well.

Finally, sometimes senior lawyers may not be good indicators of what is expected. At one firm, a junior lawyer looked to a senior lawyer who often arrived at the office at 10:30 a.m. to judge what was acceptable. The senior lawyer, however, saw his conduct as a privilege earned through hard work, and as an offset for the fact he did a lot of travel for work. Even that senior lawyer then criticized associates who arrived for work at a similar time.

The lesson here for associates is to try to determine what the law firm really expects from them. Otherwise, a lawyer may feel that his or her work habits are satisfying the need for the firms (*i.e.*, sufficient hours are being billed), while actually causing the law firm to become disappointed or frustrated with the lawyer's behavior and performance.

Billing Expectations

Many firms have "minimum billable hours." This number may not say much about a firm. Every lawyer at the firm—or at least every lawyer whom the firm wants to keep at the firm—may work far more or less than this number. Furthermore, this number will not accurately reflect how much people work (as noted, sometimes firms agree not to bill certain time or tasks), or when they are expected to work. For example, some firms continue to have unwritten "face time" requirements, where senior lawyers expect to see junior lawyers in the office at certain times—such as Saturday mornings—if the junior lawyers are serious about being promoted in the firm. A "minimum hours" requirement provides no guidance on such requirements.

If a lawyer really wants to know how much lawyers are expected to work, he or she should find out (a) how many hours are billed by lawyers who are still at the firm and are being promoted and well compensated, (b) at what level of work bonuses become available and are earned, and (c) when lawyers are expected to work. Be aware as well that certain practice groups or offices may have practices that are not consistent with expectations or requirements in other parts of the firm.

Where Client Work Ranks

Another major mistake that young lawyers make is not demonstrating an understanding that client work is very important, or sending mixed messages to partners about where the associate ranks the client's needs. To avoid sending such a message, it may be important for young lawyers to show diligence in working on client matters and to meet internal (or external) deadlines for such work.

For example, if an associate is working on a substantial filing that has a drop-deadline deadline of Wednesday, and the filing needs to be reviewed internally by one or more supervising partners as well as externally by the client, an associate who gets a draft done late Wednesday afternoon will often be seen as having mishandled the assignment. This may happen even if the draft (when finally completed) is the associate's best work.

Why? Because the associate's delay in getting the document completed will require everyone else to rush through it. Even if the associate has drafted an excellent document, perhaps this brilliant document convinces the senior lawyers they need to omit, add, or change a section. The delay in completing the draft may make such edits impossible to complete in a timely fashion.

Not only that, the draft is only part of the work that the lawyer offers as a lawyer. Good lawyers enjoy long, productive relationships with clients. A lawyer who continually gives a client documents to review at the last minute, or who requires a client to set aside the work they were doing to handle something thrust upon them by the lawyer, jeopardizes that relationship.

Thus, completing a task on time, even for an apparent arbitrary internal deadline, may be absolutely crucial. And a young lawyer may need to work very long hours to complete the task on time.

This can create problems because young lawyers, particularly young lawyers who have working spouses, may need to balance demands of work with other needs. A young lawyer who expects to leave early to pick up children from daycare or to meet some other personal need may be perceived as not fulfilling firm expectations if those obligations appear to jeopardize the ability of the lawyer or the firm to complete a task for a client in a timely fashion.

One solution to this is for the lawyer to communicate what he or she is doing, and to ensure that the deadline is met. For example, if the lawyer needs to attend a family or personal dinner, the lawyer may tell the partner that he or she is leaving for a few hours, but will return and work late to complete the task so that it will be ready before the pre-established deadline. Lawyers should also be mindful that satisfying such a deadline may require very late work, particularly since many tasks take far longer than a newer lawyer estimates.

Finally, a true story to drive this point home. A partner and associate were preparing for a significant multi-day trial some distance from their main office. The trial would start on a Monday; for our purposes, let us say that the first day of trial was March 15. Less than two weeks before trial, the associate mentioned to the partner that the associate was supposed to attend a friend's out-of-town wedding the weekend before the trial; that is, March 13–14.

The partner was furious. The associate had known about the wedding for some time, but had chosen not to tell the partner—likely because the associate recognized that the partner would replace the associate on the trial team. However, the partner expected that both the partner and associate would be preparing for trial each of the last days, including the weekend, and that they would need to travel to the trial site at minimum on Sunday, March 14, to be ready for the trial to open on Monday, March 15. By failing to tell the partner earlier, the associate successfully remained on the case—but ultimately missed the close friend's wedding.

37 Basics of Lawyers' Professional Liability Insurance

In addition to commercial general liability (CGL) insurance that most businesses—including law firms—purchase, most lawyers and law firms have some form of professional liability or malpractice insurance. The CGL insurance policy makes sure that the firm's or lawyer's resources will not be imperiled if someone has an accident while on firm property or firm business, or from similar risks that all businesses face. Most CGL insurance policies, however, expressly state that they do not cover claims arising from or related to the provision of professional services to a client of an insured law firm.

Lawyers professional liability (LPL) insurance provides coverage for claims arising from or related to the provision of professional services. Law firms or lawyers may be required to carry LPL insurance (Oregon, for example, mandates that virtually all private practice lawyers maintain lawyers professional liability insurance coverage). More often, lawyers and firms simply choose to carry LPL insurance to protect themselves from potential claims. In some jurisdictions, although LPL insurance is not required, a lawyer must report to bar authorities—and possibly to others including clients—if the lawyer does not have professional liability insurance coverage.

Virtually all LPL insurance policies today are "claims made" policies.[150] Claims-made policies cover claims made against an insured (the lawyer or firm) during the policy period. A claim is normally "made" when the lawyer or firm receives notice that a client has or intends to make a claim against the lawyer about particular legal services. Normally, claims-made policies include specific triggers on when the law firm or lawyer must provide the LPL insurer with notice of a potential claim, and a period of time when such notice must be provided. If a law firm fails to provide notice of the claim during the specified period, the insurer may have no obligation to defend or indemnify the law firm on that claim.

Claims-made policies cover all legal services provided after a certain date, as long as the lawyer learns of the claim during the policy period. A claims-made policy also normally requires a lawyer or firm to disclose all claims or potential claims known at the time LPL insurance is sought on the policy application. These claims are then generally excluded from coverage.

Finally, particularly if a law firm or lawyer is ceasing practice or changing firms, a lawyer or firm may be able to purchase "tail coverage" that will provide insurance for claims that are made against the firm or lawyer after a claims-made policy ends. Thus, if a lawyer purchases a claims-made LPL insurance policy, and the term of that policy covers the 2010 policy year, the policy would cover any claims made against the lawyer relating to work done after a particular date, say January 1, 2008, as long as the lawyer first received notice of the claim in 2010. If a lawyer or firm first learned of the claim on or after January 1, 2011, there would be no coverage under the 2010 "claims made" policy, even if the claim related to work performed in 2010. Law firms or lawyers typically

[150]The other type of LPL insurance policy is an "occurrence" policy. These policies cover claims made for services provided during the policy period, without regard for when the lawyer receives notice of the claim.

purchase consecutive policies or renew claims-made policies to prevent such gaps in coverage. Alternatively, if the lawyer or firm ceased practice at the end of 2010, or changed firms and joined a firm whose policy would not cover work at the prior firm, the lawyer or firm might purchase a tail policy in case any claims are made after December 31, 2010, perhaps for a period equal to the statute of limitations for a legal malpractice claim.

Professional liability insurance policies commonly specify what firm actions and damages will and will not be covered. Intentional misconduct such as a lawyer defrauding a client, punitive damages, and fee disputes generally do not receive coverage. In addition, a policy may not cover claims where a law firm lawyer served the claimant as an officer or director, or where a firm lawyer owned a specified portion of the claimant, or where the claim arises out of the provision of non-legal services. Insurance polices may also require certain cooperation from an insured. If the insured fails to provide the required cooperation, this may cause the insured firm to forfeit its right to defense and indemnification from the insured.

A claim against an insured firm will often trigger a duty for the insurer to defend the insured and also a duty to indemnify the insured. The duty to defend (*i.e.*, to retain legal counsel and try to resolve the claim) is generally broader than the duty to indemnify the insured (*i.e.*, pay damages or a settlement arising from a claim). This often results in the insurer hiring or (where the insured can select counsel) paying for a lawyer to defend the insured against claims, even if the insured firm may not have LPL insurance coverage for such claims. For example, an insurer may have a duty to defend a lawsuit that alleges both professional malpractice and fraud, but a duty to indemnify only for damages paid on account of the malpractice claim.

When a claim includes both covered and uncovered claims or damages, the insurance company may send a "reservation of rights" letter that specifies the insurer is defending and may even settle a claim, but may reserve its right to seek repayment for all or a portion of the fees and expenses if some or all claims ultimately relate to actions or damages the insurance policy does not cover.

Often an insurance policy will have a limit on how much can be paid on a single claim, and how much can be paid for all claims that arise during the policy period. These amounts normally include payments made both to legal counsel defending the firm and also payments made to those making claims against the firm. Therefore, if a lawyer has $500,000 in professional liability insurance coverage, and the insurer incurs $300,000 in legal fees to defend the claim, the insured will be required to pay any amount of a judgment or settlement that exceeds $200,000 (the $500,000 in coverage less the $300,000 in fees). Also, most policies require the lawyer to pay a deductible, perhaps the first $2,500 or $5,000 in costs incurred on a claim in defense, settlement, judgment, or the like. Thus, a law firm may bear complete responsibility for very small claims brought against the firm. Very large firms often have very large deductibles, also called "self-insured retentions," that may require the firm to cover all claims-related costs until those costs exceed perhaps $100,000 or $1,000,000 or more.

Firms vary greatly regarding how much insurance coverage they carry, and how much such coverage costs. A history of past claims, or participation in certain types of practices deemed higher risk, may also increase the costs for professional liability insurance. *Law Firm, Inc.* estimates, for example, that Am Law 200 firms—that is, the 200 most profitable large firms based in the United States—spend approximately $6,000-8,000 per lawyer on professional liability insurance each year, plus approximately $1,600 on commercial general insurance or property and casualty insurance. Such firms probably have several million dollars of coverage available for each claim, but they also may have large deductibles ($100,000 or more) before an insurance provider assumes the costs of defense or resolving the claims.

Dealing with Mistakes

38

At some point during a legal career, virtually every lawyer is going to make a real mistake. This is not a reference to a minor, inconsequential mistake, like a basic typographical error that has no impact on anything. This section refers to a serious mistake, one that could impact a client or the firm in a serious manner. This may involve filing a lawsuit and then learning it has no merit, missing a deadline for some crucial action, or preparing a contract or will and only later learning that the document lacked some key provision. This section attempts to provide guidance for how a newer lawyer should deal with such a mistake.

Most lawyers have personalities that cause them to seek to avoid all mistakes. When a lawyer does make such a mistake, the lawyer may have difficulty recognizing and accepting it. Or the lawyer may try to rationalize the mistake away, to blame it on someone else, or to conceal it.[151] None of these responses, however, involves trying to address or fix the mistake.

---

[151]Carolyn Elefant, *When Lawyers Make Mistakes*, Law.com (Feb. 7, 2005), *available at* **http://www.law.com/jsp/law/sfb/lawArticleSFB.jsp?id=1107550994257**.

Instead, the following five steps are suggested for dealing with a real mistake:

First, the lawyer should confirm that he or she really did make the mistake. The lawyers should spend a short amount of time—perhaps an hour or two, generally, not a few days—assessing what happened. The lawyer should confirm that the expected evidence does not exist, that the deadline was missed, or that the document omitted the key provision. The lawyer should gather the relevant documents, check the court file, and otherwise investigate and determine what happened.

Second, the lawyer should enlist help at least initially from another lawyer, particularly a trusted senior lawyer at the firm or someone who has served as a mentor or guide to the lawyer. Perhaps the most difficult task for all lawyers, and particularly newer lawyers, is to realize that they should not have exclusive ownership over the mistake and how to fix it. They should expect to share the mistake with someone who can provide wisdom, guidance, and a different perspective on the issue. A lawyer more removed from the mistake will likely have a more objective perspective, and perhaps a better vantage point to assess and offer a resolution of how to deal with the problem. A more experienced lawyer may also know how others have fixed the same or a similar problem.

So whom should the lawyer tell about the mistake? There are likely up to three lawyers that the lawyer who learned of the mistake may want or need to notify:

1. A formal or informal mentor at the firm, or another more senior lawyer whom the lawyer trusts will help the lawyer recognizing the problem in additional disclosure to address the problem;
2. The firm's ethics or risk management counsel (see Chapter 41), or other lawyer at the firm who is particularly good at listening to and evaluating problems, and coming up with possible resolutions for such problems; and
3. The supervising attorney or client-relationship attorney, who will likely be a necessary participant in any effort to notify the client of or fix a potential problem.

The aim is to enlist allies who will help provide notice and offer possible solutions to other lawyers and ultimately, as appropriate, the client.

A lawyer realizing a mistake may realize additional people can and should receive notice. For example, the lawyer may need to notify firm management or the relevant practice group leader. The lawyer reporting the mistake should also take care in considering whom to avoid notifying, at least before all facts are known. For example, while it is always difficult to confront a powerful senior partner with allegations of wrongdoing, to do so alone and relying upon incomplete and inaccurate or misunderstood facts can have serious consequences for a more junior lawyer.

After determining whom to tell, the lawyer should also consider how to tell the other, often more senior, lawyers about the mistake. Often it is good to try to think about the problem and have a suggested possible solution or solutions ready for discussion. This demonstrates the lawyer providing notice has taken ownership of the problem and is trying to resolve it. Thus, the lawyer likely should avoid saying simply, "We failed to provide the required notice." Instead, the lawyer providing notice would likely be better served to say, "I realized that our deadline for filing notice was yesterday. I know we want to provide notice. Do you want me to . . . ?" The senior lawyer may reject the suggested course of action, but at least this formula starts the dialogue with a focus on how to properly resolve the issue. Such a discussion should also be in person if at all possible, and the lawyer providing notice should have copies of the relevant documents, rules, and other resources available for each lawyer expected to participate in the particular discussion.

Third, the lawyer—now acting with assistance of other allies at the firm—should attempt to formulate a possible resolution or list of possible solutions for the problem. Working to formulate such a plan demonstrates that the lawyer has taken responsibility for the problem, and is acting to try to resolve it properly.

Preparing alternatives to address or resolve a problem should not be an excuse for lengthy delay. Also, the firm should not undertake any action that operates to the detriment of a client unless the client is informed fully and consents to such course of action.

Therefore, if a firm realizes it missed an important deadline, say for filing a responsive pleading, it should not try to resolve the matter without client knowledge in the hopes this will avoid further disclosure to or questions from the client.

If a senior lawyer's solution seems unethical or improper, a junior lawyer should make sure the junior lawyer fully understands the senior lawyer's position. On several occasions, I have become involved in situations when junior lawyers believed a senior lawyer was acting inappropriately, only to learn that either the junior or senior lawyer misunderstand the underlying situation or proposed solution. Further, the junior lawyer should realize that, even when acting at the direction of a supervising lawyer, under ABA Model Rule 5.2 a junior lawyer generally must still ensure his or her conduct satisfies all ethical obligations.

Fourth, when a problem relates to and materially affects the client, the law firm should notify the client of the problem and, as appropriate, possible means for resolving the problem. Ethical obligations, for example under ABA Model Rule 1.4, and concurrent fiduciary obligations may compel a law firm to notify a client affected by the firm's mistake. Even if not compelled, client notice may be appropriate or necessary to maintain good client relations. Hopefully one or more senior lawyers from the firm will make or accompany a junior lawyer forced to make such a call, to demonstrate their support for and faith in the junior lawyer. When such a call is made, the lawyers should take care before admitting liability, offering a settlement, or the like. Admitting liability may void coverage under the lawyers' professional liability policy. An offer to settle a claim with a client, meanwhile, may be subject to additional regulations, in particular those contained in a state's version of ABA Model Rule 1.8(h).

Dealing with Potential Malpractice or Third-Party Claims

When a mistake may have caused damage to a client or third party, the potential lawyer liability or malpractice claim adds additional wrinkles to the proper handling. Ordinarily a lawyer's or firm's professional liability policy requires a lawyer or firm to promptly provide notice of a potential for that claim to be covered. Such notice may need to be in writing. A lawyer should consult the policy to ensure that the lawyer satisfies all notice requirements. When the firm has a risk management counsel, that risk management counsel will likely have access to the necessary information for providing notice to the insurer, and ordinarily should be involved in the process.

When an insurer receives notice of a claim or potential claim, it may provide a lawyer or firm with additional resources in an effort to mitigate or avoid a claim. Many insurers, for example, have risk management counsel available to provide guidance or to offer possible solutions to a problem. Thus, prompt reporting may be a prudent course of action, although it may also increase premiums, another factor that may deserve consideration.

In addition, professional liability policies often provide that a lawyer or firm waives coverage if the lawyer or firm confesses liability or enters a settlement with the impacted party. Such considerations may make it appropriate to contact the insurer before contacting the client to discuss the potential issue or to admit a mistake was made and that a malpractice claim may be available. If a lawyer or firm makes such a confession of guilt, this may cause the lawyer or firm to lose all insurance coverage on that claim.

Finally, if there is a potential malpractice claim, realize that this might have a necessary impact on the representation as well as how the lawyers handle themselves. Everyone with whom the involved lawyers talk may become potential witnesses. Every document written about the issue may also become a potential exhibit. Thus, it may be better for a lawyer to put as little as possible in the email. If you are emailing risk management counsel, say simply, "I need to speak with you promptly. Call me." Do not put all the facts in an email, or send an email saying, "I committed malpractice by missing the deadline for filing a notice of appeal in the Jones case. Call me to discuss."

Additionally, if a lawyer or firm has committed malpractice, this may cause a conflict that may impair the firm's continued handling of the matter. For example, if a plaintiff's lawyer omits a claim or fails to file a timely notice of appeal, and the time for filing that claim or appeal has expired, the fact that the plaintiff's lawyer promptly thereafter negotiates and enters a settlement without telling the client about the missed deadline may be seen—including by a judge or jury—as a self-serving act intended to avoid malpractice liability. This, in turn, may be a reason that judgment is subsequently entered against the plaintiff's counsel for malpractice.

Dealing with Sanctions Motions and Disciplinary Complaints

In litigation today, motions for sanctions have become somewhat more commonplace. And in some practices—notably consumer-focused practices like divorce and criminal law—ethics or disciplinary complaints have become rather commonplace (often filed by the opposing party). This is unfortunate. This also means there is a good chance that a litigation attorney will be the subject of a sanctions motion or disciplinary complaint at some point in his or her career, particularly if the lawyer has a consumer-focused practice.

Sanctions motions and disciplinary complaints do not necessarily require any special treatment different from the preceding discussion of addressing mistakes. Having devoted a significant portion of my practice to discipline and sanctions issues, however, I want to offer four suggestions:

First, the lawyer accused of misconduct should always enlist an uninvolved lawyer to review a response before it is submitted. This will often allow the accused lawyer to avoid unnecessarily complicating the situation, and also provide that the accused lawyer's emotions do not unnecessarily taint and thus weaken the response.

Second, as a general matter, the lawyer will be well served by avoiding an attack on the accuser as a means of defense. Often the best approach is to end a fight arising out of ethics or sanctions rules as soon as possible. A response that attacks the other side may only complicate a situation, causing disciplinary counsel or a judge to take greater note of the initial filing, or to believe that perhaps an entire situation requires further investigation or a hearing.

Third, the accused lawyer should consider providing notice to his or her lawyer's professional liability insurer. As noted earlier, a lawyer often has an obligation to provide the insurer with notice when the lawyer knows or should know of a claim. A motion for sanctions or disciplinary complaint may trigger such a duty to provide notice. Also, some LPL policies provide funds for a lawyer to retain counsel to assist with a response to a disciplinary complaint or, less frequently, a motion for sanctions or similar pleading.

Finally, under virtually no circumstances should a lawyer ignore a motion for sanctions or disciplinary complaint. Sanctions motions and disciplinary complaints do not wither and die if ignored. In fact, a lawyer may face more serious penalties if the lawyer fails to respond to a motion for sanctions or disciplinary complaint.

Diversity in Law Firms

39

Many law firms continue to struggle with diversity. As discussed earlier, many firms feel (or are overtly under) significant pressure—particularly from clients—to retain and promote diverse attorneys. For a variety of reasons, some legitimate, some not, many firms struggle with addressing even this threshold issue.

Further, when attorneys of diverse racial backgrounds are at a firm, some firms and diverse attorneys struggle with how to make this relationship meaningful. In 2006, the ABA completed a study titled *Visible Invisibility: Women of Color in Law Firms*. This study reported evidence of widespread discrimination against female lawyers of color. "Nearly half (49 percent) said they'd been subjected to demeaning comments or other types of harassment."[152] Lawyer's stories were shocking, including the following:

[152]Ari Shapiro, *Why So Few Minority Women Stay at Law Firms,* All Things Considered (Aug. 3, 2006), *available at* **http://www.npr.org/templates/story/story.php?storyId=5613964**. This article also explains that "[t]he ABA report uses the phrase 'of color' as an umbrella term for persons who are Hispanic/Latina, African-American, Native American, Asian-American and those from multiracial backgrounds." *Id.*

> "I had a managing partner call me into his office when I was a fourth-year [associate]. He introduced me to the client who was Korean and he tells him that I'm Korean, too. He says, 'She eats kim chee, just like you.' He said to me, 'Talk to him.' I looked at the client and said, 'It's a pleasure to meet you. I'm sure you speak English better than I speak Korean.' The client's face was so red. Then the partner left a message on my internal message system, and he was speaking gibberish, trying to sound like an Asian speaker. I called every partner on my floor and said, 'You need to come and listen to this.' I played that message 10 times. Ten times."[153]

> "I felt like an exotic animal. I was always asked to attend functions and award ceremonies, speak to law students of color, and pose for advertising publications. However, I never had contact with partners in power other than at these events. Law firms would do well to examine whether their associates of color are given real opportunities to interact with the power structure of the firm."[154]

Often these comments effectively center around a sense that the diverse lawyer is being included to provide diversity, but not for a real personal contribution. "When diversity was an asset to landing a government contract or eliciting new business from clients of color I was included in client meetings, but not otherwise."[155]

What is the solution? As in the next Chapter, mentoring is often considered a key factor in determining what a lawyer will do and whether a lawyer will advance at a firm. Recognizing this reality, many firms have special programs, often mentoring programs, for diverse lawyers. Sometimes these programs can be quite good. Other times, they may just be window dressing. The key solution for a newer attorney is often to identify a champion, protector, and mentor, through a formal mentoring program or otherwise. This senior lawyer can make sure the newer diverse lawyer receives good work opportunities and has an advocate discussed including during important compensation and promotion meetings.

[153] *Id.*
[154] *Id.*
[155] *Id.*

Unfortunately, the ABA report makes clear that for women of color, this can be quite difficult. Anecdotes from diverse male lawyers suggest they face many of the same problems. Studies of Harvard Law School graduates of color conducted by David Wilkins and Mitu Gulati support this premise. They report:

> Associates who do not find themselves on the training track [likely to lead to promotion] have three options: (i) they can leave immediately; (ii) they can attempt to move themselves onto the training track; or (iii) they can stay at the firm but invest their time and energy in developing non-firm-specific skills that will help them get another job. Which of these strategies a given associate will pursue depends upon both the likelihood that she can change her reputation within the firm and her prospects in the external employment market. . . .
>
> Black associates face three significant barriers to getting on the training track. First, they are less likely than whites to find mentors who will give them challenging work and provide them with advice and counseling about how to succeed at the firm. Second, they face higher costs from making mistakes than their white peers. Third, their future employment prospects with other elite firms diminish more rapidly than those of similarly situated associates. . . .
>
> In order to get on the training track, an associate has to have mentors among the firm's partners or senior associates who can provide the Royal Jelly of good training. Blacks consistently report that they have difficulty in forming these supportive relationships. . . . [I]n our survey of black Harvard Law School graduates, less than 40% of those surveyed . . . stated that a partner had taken interest in their work or their career. Sixty-eight percent of those who did not find a mentor . . . stated that this was a significant factor in their decision to leave the firm."[156]

---

[156]David Wilkins & Mitu Gulati, *Why Are There So Few Black Lawyers in Corporate Law Firms? An Institutional Analysis*, 84 Cal. L. Rev. 493, 567-68 (1996); *see also* David Wilkins & Mitu Gulati, *Reconceiving the Tournament of Lawyers: Tracking, Seeding, and Information Control in the Internal Labor Markets of Elite Law Firms*, 84 Va. L. Rev . 1581 (1998).

Efforts by firms and clients may be addressing some of the situations, including improving employment prospects at elite firms. But anecdotal information available to me suggests many firms have a long way to go before they should consider the special problems facing diverse attorneys resolved.

40 Mentoring

Mentoring is generally accepted as one of the most important tools for teaching newer lawyers how to practice and behave in practice, and for helping them be successful in the practice of law. Opportunities for newer lawyers to obtain such mentoring, however, vary greatly.

Some firms devote considerable resources into mentoring, and assign mentors to every associate—or perhaps every or virtually every lawyer—at the firm. (Mentoring programs that pair senior and junior female or diverse attorneys are also common.) The mentoring programs may require regular meetings between a mentor and protégé. A firm may also devote resources to such activities, such as providing special programs for mentors and protégés, budgets to finance breakfast or lunch at such meetings, or treating some or all time spent on mentoring as a billable activity. A firm may also consider the quality of a senior lawyer's efforts at mentoring as a factor in setting that senior lawyer's compensation.

Other firms have little or no formal mentoring program. Sometimes these firms may also assign a senior lawyer to a newer lawyer, but provide few other resources, oversight, or structure. Or the firm may be totally silent on mentoring.

Firms also vary with regard to the quality of mentoring, regardless of what resources they invest in a mentoring program. Sometimes the firm with the comprehensive, expensive program receives significant benefits in associate retention and performance through that program. Other times, such a program seems to provide little or no significant benefit to the firm, or to the quality of life or opportunities for firm associates. At other firms, active mentoring may be occurring outside or absent a formal mentoring program because a few senior lawyers or the broader firm culture ensure that newer lawyers receive significant mentoring, opportunities, and feedback.

Regardless of what opportunities a firm presents, it is generally agreed that as a group, newer lawyers need mentors to develop themselves and their practices. Often a newer lawyer can arrange a formal or informal mentoring relationship with a more senior lawyer at his or her firm. Also, many state and local bar associations have mentoring programs that will pair senior and newer lawyers who practice in the same field or locality. A newer lawyer who wants to make a private law career rewarding would be well served by seeking a mentor through these or other means.

The mentor should be someone who can help the lawyer with the substantive practice of law, but also with practice management issues including those discussed in this book. Sometimes a newer lawyer may find it is best to have multiple mentors, including someone to help with firm politics, someone to assist with substantive matters, and someone outside the firm to advise on career development issues.

41 Supervision and Risk Management

In addition to formal or informal mentoring programs, firms sometimes establish some system for supervising newer lawyers. A supervising attorney may be a practice group leader or mentor, or some other senior lawyer responsible for making sure that a newer lawyer has enough work and is otherwise complying with the firm's and other relevant standards. ABA Model Rule 5.1—and with regard to nonlawyer staff Rule 5.3—generally require some form of supervision of newer lawyers.[157] Firms may also use a nonlawyer to supervise associate work-loads, opportunities, and the like.

In addition, the growth of law firms and the increase in the sophistication and operation of law firms has led many firms to designate a law firm general counsel, ethics counsel, or risk management counsel. These titles may indicate different responsi-

---

[157]Senior lawyers may also face discipline if they fail to provide adequate supervision to more junior lawyers. *See, e.g., Attorney Grievance Commission of Maryland v. Kimmel*, 955 A.2d 269 (Md. 2008).

bilities: the general counsel is normally a firm's chief legal officer, with responsibility for all legal matters impacting the firm (such as real estate, employment, and contract issues), while the ethics counsel may focus on ethics issues (conflicts and conflict waivers) and the risk management counsel may focus mainly on avoiding or managing malpractice or other claims against the firm. Often, however, a lawyer or in some instances a group of lawyers may have some or all of these responsibilities, regardless of the exact title used. Virtually all large law firms have someone designated to handle such responsibilities, and even smaller firms often have someone formally or informally recognized as the person to handle ethics or other issues.

When a firm has an ethics or risk management counsel, this person may be designated as the person who should receive, investigate, and address allegations of misconduct involving firm lawyers and staff. For newer lawyers at a firm, such a person may serve as an important person to contact should the newer lawyer encounter professional or other difficulties at a firm. If a newer lawyer observes improper billing or lawyer misconduct or suffers harassment, for example, that newer lawyer may need to report these issues to the law firm's general counsel. Such reporting may initiate a proper response.

Conclusion

Law firms offer newer lawyers some of the best and the worst aspects of the practice of law. A law firm practice can be filled with opportunity and excitement, or boredom. It can be personally and financially rewarding, or personally and financially devastating. This text has attempted to offer some of the texture of various firms, and to help provide a framework so that you can understand a firm where you may interview or work, and to compare that firm with others.

If you find anything this text failed to discuss, or have particular experiences or observations that you want us to know, please feel free to contact the author Michael Downey at Hinshaw & Culbertson, LLP.

Good luck and may your law firm experience be everything good you desire and more.

Finis

Index

iPad in One Hour for Lawyers, Second Edition

By Tom Mighell

Product Code: 5110747 • **LP Price:** $24.95 • **Regular Price:** $39.95

Whether you are a new or a more advanced iPad user, *iPad in One Hour for Lawyers* takes a great deal of the mystery and confusion out of using your iPad. Ideal for lawyers who want to get up to speed swiftly, this book presents the essentials so you don't get bogged down in technical jargon and extraneous features and apps. In just six, short lessons, you'll learn how to:

- Quickly Navigate and Use the iPad User Interface
- Set Up Mail, Calendar, and Contacts
- Create and Use Folders to Multitask and Manage Apps
- Add Files to Your iPad, and Sync Them
- View and Manage Pleadings, Case Law, Contracts, and other Legal Documents
- Use Your iPad to Take Notes and Create Documents
- Use Legal-Specific Apps at Trial or in Doing Research

Personal Branding In One Hour for Lawyers

By Katy Goshtasbi

Product Code: 5110765 • **LP Price:** $39.95 • **Regular Price:** $49.95

With over 1.2 million licensed attorneys in the United States, how do lawyers stand out from their fellow practitioners and get jobs, promotions, clients, and referrals? To survive and thrive, lawyers must develop their own intentional personal brand to distinguish themselves from the competition. In Personal Branding in One Hour for Lawyers, personal branding expert and experienced attorney Katy Goshtasbi explains how attorneys can highlight their unique talents and abilities, manage their perceptions, and achieve greater success as a lawyer in the process. In just one hour, you will learn to:

- Discover your personal brand--and why it matters to colleagues and clients
- Use your personal brand as a marketing tool
- Stand out from the crowd--improve your visual brand by making simple, yet impactful, changes to your attire and personal appearance
- Create effective marketing materials for your brand
- Network successfully to implement your personal brand
- Communicate your brand effectively

The Lawyer's Guide to Professional Coaching

By Andrew Elowitt

Product Code: 5110735 • **LP Price:** $47.95 • **Regular Price:** $79.95

Become more efficient and profitable in your law practice by employing a professional coach. The Lawyer's Guide to Professional Coaching will teach you to find, select, and work productively with the right coach for your needs--and transform your practice in the process. Learn how to get the most out of coaching, decide whether coaching is right for you and your firm, and use coaching skills when you manage, mentor, and collaborate with client and colleagues.

Lessons in Leadership: Essential Skills for Lawyers

By Thomas C. Grella

Product Code: 5110761 • **LP Price:** $47.95 • **Regular Price:** $79.95

More lawyers than ever before are using Twitter to network with colleagues, attract clients, market their law firms, and even read the news. But to the uninitiated, Twitter's short messages, or tweets, can seem like they are written in a foreign language. Twitter in One Hour for Lawyers will demystify one of the most important social-media platforms of our time and teach you to tweet like an expert. In just one hour, you will learn to:

- Create a Twitter account and set up your profile
- Read tweets and understand Twitter jargon
- Write tweets—and send them at the appropriate time
- Gain an audience—follow and be followed
- Engage with other Twitters users
- Integrate Twitter into your firm's marketing plan
- Cross-post your tweets with other social media platforms like Facebook and LinkedIn
- Understand the relevant ethics, privacy, and security concerns
- Get the greatest possible return on your Twitter investment

Virtual Law Practice: How to Deliver Legal Services Online

By Stephanie L. Kimbro

Product Code: 5110707 • **LP Price:** $47.95 • **Regular Price:** $79.95

The legal market has recently experienced a dramatic shift as lawyers seek out alternative methods of practicing law and providing more affordable legal services. Virtual law practice is revolutionizing the way the public receives legal services and how legal professionals work with clients. If you are interested in this form of practicing law, *Virtual Law Practice* will help you:

- Responsibly deliver legal services online to your clients
- Successfully set up and operate a virtual law office
- Establish a virtual law practice online through a secure, client-specific portal
- Manage and market your virtual law practice
- Understand state ethics and advisory opinions
- Find more flexibility and work/life balance in the legal profession

The Lawyer's Essential Guide to Writing

By Marie Buckley

Product Code: 5110726 • **LP Price:** $47.95 • **Regular Price:** $79.95

This is a readable, concrete guide to contemporary legal writing. Based on Marie Buckley's years of experience coaching lawyers, this book provides a systematic approach to all forms of written communication, from memoranda and briefs to e-mail and blogs. The book sets forth three principles for powerful writing and shows how to apply those principles to develop a clean and confident style.

30-DAY RISK-FREE ORDER FORM

ABA LAW PRACTICE DIVISION
The Business of Practicing Law

'lease print or type. To ship UPS, we must have your street address.
' you list a P.O. Box, we will ship by U.S. Mail.

lame

lember ID

irm/Organization

treet Address

ity/State/Zip

rea Code/Phone (In case we have a question about your order)

-mail

lethod of Payment:

☐ Check enclosed, payable to American Bar Association

☐ MasterCard ☐ Visa ☐ American Express

ard Number Expiration Date

ignature Required

MAIL THIS FORM TO:
American Bar Association, Publication Orders
P.O. Box 10892, Chicago, IL 60610

ORDER BY PHONE:
24 hours a day, 7 days a week:
Call 1-800-285-2221 to place a credit card order. We accept Visa, MasterCard, and American Express.

EMAIL ORDERS: orders@americanbar.org
FAX ORDERS: 1-312-988-5568

VISIT OUR WEB SITE: www.ShopABA.org
Allow 7-10 days for regular UPS delivery. Need it sooner? Ask about our overnight delivery options. Call the ABA Service Center at 1-800-285-2221 for more information.

GUARANTEE:
If–for any reason–you are not satisfied with your purchase, you may return it within 30 days of receipt for a refund of the price of the book(s). No questions asked.

Thank You For Your Order.

Join the ABA Law Practice Division today and receive a substantial discount on Division publications!

roduct Code:	Description:	Quantity:	Price:	Total Price:
				$
				$
				$
				$
				$

Shipping/Handling:

.00 to $9.99	add $0.00
0.00 to $49.99	add $5.95
0.00 to $99.99	add $7.95
00.00 to $199.99	add $9.95
00.00 to $499.99	add $12.95

***Tax:**
IL residents add 9.25%
DC residents add 5.75%

Subtotal:	$
***Tax:**	$
****Shipping/Handling:**	$
Yes, I am an ABA member and would like to join the Law Practice Division today! (Add $50.00)	$
Total:	$